Schuylkill

Valley

Journal

Volume 43
Fall 2016

The *Schuylkill Valley Journal* is published twice a year

Patrons of the Schuylkill Valley Journal
(contributions of $50 or more)

Bill Ehrhart
Richard Krok
Suzanne Marinell
Fran Metzman
Edmund B. Spaeth, Jr.
Laura Ulmer
Bill Wunder

Peter Krok
Claire Magee
Bernadette McBride
Richard Moyer
Robert Spreter
Shirley Wood

Subscriptions: Single Issue: $10 and $13 (if mailing is included)
1 year: $23 (includes mailing)
2 years: $45 (includes mailing)

For submission guidelines:
See page 230 for a complete list of guidelines.

Cover photo: Lou McKee
Photographer: Robin Hiteshew

Schuylkill Valley Journal

Founding Editor	Jim Marinell
Editor-in-Chief	Peter Krok
Managing Editor	Mark Danowsky
Assistant Managing Editor	Kelli Wilhelm
Co-Poetry Editor	Bill Wunder
Co-Poetry Editor	Bernadette McBride
Fiction Editor	Fran Metzman
Arts Editor	David Kozinski
Contributing Writer	Mike Cohen
Contributing Writer	Ray Greenblatt
Production Editor	Don Philbrick
Online Architect/Producer	Jordan Heil
Social Media Coordinator	Brenna Ritzert
Graphic Designer	Eric Sauermelch
	ericsour@gmail.com

The *Schuylkill Valley Journal* is available online at
www.svjlit.com

Contents
Volume 43, Fall 2016

Tributes to Lou McKee

Essays by Lou McKee

Poetry by Lou McKee

Poetry

Poetry Continued

Fiction

Philadelphia Sculpture

Non-Fiction

CELEBRATING THE POET
LOU MCKEE
July 31, 1951—November 25, 2011

I sent out word that I would like to do a special celebration of Lou McKee on the fifth anniversary of his death. The outcome is this special issue of the *Schuylkill Valley Journal* offers a tribute to Lou McKee, the man, his work, and also includes acknowledgments to Lou, some of his poetry and some of his articles

Who was Lou McKee? He was a fiercely dedicated and intense poet who had a remarkable impact on many of the poets in the area (in fact an area from Philadelphia to San Francisco). One could call him a patron spirit of poetry; his motivation was always the word, the poem and the cause. He was a generous and proud man who celebrated his Irish heritage and who never had much income, but he knew poetry and poets and publications.

He was a regular on *The Writer's Almanac* with Garrison Keillor. His poems and reviews were published in numerous journals and anthologies. Lou was a fixture of the Philadelphia poetry scene beginning in the early 1970s. He was the author of *Schuylkill County* (Wampeter, 1982), *The True Speed of Things* (Slash and Burn, 1984), and fourteen other collections. More recently, he published *River Architecture: Poems from Here & There 1973-1993* (Cynic, 1999), *Loose Change* (Marsh River Editions, 2001), and a volume in the Pudding House *Greatest Hits* series. Gerald Stern called his work "heart-breaking" and "necessary." Naomi Shihab Nye wrote, "Louis McKee is one of the truest hearts and voices in poetry we will ever be lucky to know." One can find quite a lot by searching the internet and checking Wikipedia.

For several years Lou was an editor of the *Painted Bride Quarterly* (approx. 1988 – 1994). He brought out a number of special issue; two issues highlighted the work of Etheridge Knight and John Logan. In 1996 he became the editor of *One Trick Pony* which at that time was the best poetry journal in the region. He carried it on by himself as long as he could; until 2007 when funds and body could no longer maintain the effort. The twelve issues of *One Trick Pony* include the following poets: Lynn Levin, Harry Humes, Gerald Stern, W. D. Ehrhart, Will Inman, Willian Heyen, Billy Collins, Jared Carter, Tina Barr, Philip Dacey, Paul Muldoon, Vivian Shipley, Simon Perchik, Jeanne Murray Walker, Len Roberts, Daniel Hoffman, Denise Duhamel, Philip Dacey, Susan Terris, Afaa M. Weaver, Naomi Shihab Nye, and many more. I am fortunate to have my work included among the many well-known contributors to *One Trick Pony*.

In 2010, the year before he died, Lou wrote an essay which appeared in the *Schuylkill Valley Journal* (Volume 31), "Charlie, Wasn't That a Time," about a heyday of poetry in Philadelphia. It was the late 1970's and early 1980's and poets used to meet at C.K. Williams' workshop at the downtown Philadelphia "Y." Some of the remarkable writers who gathered were: Sonia Sanchez, Stephen Berg, Jeanne Murray Walker, Elaine Terranova, Susan Stewart, Amy Small-McKinney, Deborah Burnham, Darcy Cummings. Read the article, you'll read about C. K. Williams and that remarkable time for poetry in Philly.

Here is a personal note that gives a glimpse into Lou's biting frankness. Years ago, he told me I wasn't writing poetry in a natural voice. As for natural voice, I think one could call it a conversational and speaking voice. Useful examples of this conversational style are Stephen Dunn and Ed Ochester. Lou's comment about my work was bitter news. I took Lou's word to heart, but it was honest and it was Lou – and Lou was really doing it for my own good. I came to realize my writing was quite different and out of kilter with contemporary poetry. I admit that the poetry I read was mostly rooted in in Louis Untermeyer's *A Treasury of Great Poems* and the poetry of William Butler Yeats and Rainer Maria Rilke. I'd like to think one's poetry got better after meeting and reading Lou.

It is clear that Lou could have lived longer if he devoted more time to his health matters, but his zeal for poetry was the constant focus of his life and his health and livelihood suffered for it. Lou knew hardship and the black dog barked in his yard, but he carried on in spite of it. He found Jameson a suitable companion at times, and he always enjoyed a conversation about poetry.

He was admirable and cantankerous and noble in his way and he had a penetrating stare. Some years ago I asked him to write an article on a Featured Poet. He read the material and said he couldn't write an article about a poet's work that he couldn't understand. Lou could be a harsh critic, but he was always honest.

Once quite expectedly he sent me a check for $110 to support the *Schuylkill Valley Journal*. Now Lou was poor enough and he could have used the money for himself but he supported journals because, so to speak, he practiced what he believed in. He felt it was the job of the poet to give to the cause. This giving was more than lip service; giving meant buying a copy and paying for a subscription. He knew how painstakingly hard it is to get more than word of mouth support. He gave because he believed it was the job of the writer. He exemplifies this commitment in his article "The Bargain" which was the last piece he sent me. "The Bargain" should be read by every writer.

I asked Lou what was his favorite sport. I was surprised by his answer. He answered pro basketball because he liked the drama of the big men on the court. He told me that Etheridge Knight used to stay at his place off and on when he was in Philly. Lou did a special retrospective of Knight's work "Etheridge Knight: A Celebration" in the *Painted Bride Quarterly* (1988) when Lou was one of the editors of that journal (approx. 1988-1991) Lou got a letter from Richard Hugo, the well-known writer of *The Triggering Town*. Hugo was impressed with Lou's book, *Schuylkill County* (published in 1982), and he was going to write a review of it, but not long after Hugo sent Lou that letter, he died on October 22, 1982. This was one of the most unfortunate events in Lou's life as a writer.

Here is a fortunate event. Lou's poem "To My Son," appeared in *APR* and as a result he was invited to read and be interviewed by Alex Chadwick on NPR's Morning Edition. (Morning Edition is the most listened to morning radio program in America.) Here is that poem:

TO MY SON

I could talk about hunger,
and the pain, thank god,
we have never had to know.
I could point to the birds, plain
as everything else in Pennsylvania,
but happy enough with their song.
Sitting on the steps each night,
even when it is too cold, we could talk
while we broke the leftover bread

into pieces the small singing mouths
would have no trouble with,
that they could carry with them
to the trees and wires where they are
thankful but offer no thanks. I could
talk to a son about these things,
but tonight I am sitting in the cold
with a dog who isn't interested
in all that, who would like to go
for the bread, or better yet, the birds,
as gray and common as they are.

The irony is that Lou did not have a son. One feels in this poem intense sincerity, understated emotion and his deep appreciation for a plain spoken language. He had a deeply personal voice in his poetry. Lou was the Featured Poet in the *Schuylkill Valley Journal* in the Spring 2007 issue (Volume 24). "The Art of Louis McKee" by Philip Dacey is included in this issue.

Lou knew many poets made clear by the poets he published and the eulogies he received at a memorial reading in Media that was coordinated by Eileen D'Angelo, the president of the Mad Poet's Society and Lou's very special friend. She became his invaluable and best friend and his real connection to what was going on in poetry in the area. Included in this issue are tributes that were written for that memorial reading.

After writing this, I realize that Lou deserves more than what is here in the SVJ but I feel comforted knowing at least he has this. My introductory piece here is a small measure in appreciation of Lou McKee. I have found in writing this that there is so much more I have discovered about Lou. In gathering my thoughts, I have further realized how very exceptional Lou is as a poet, and if I might add, I couldn't help but feeling tears.

Lou was always probing pieces of himself. Goethe wrote that he saw his works as "fragments of a great confession." In many ways I see Lou's work this way.

Lou was a big man with a big voice and a bigger heart. Above all he is a poet worth remembering and celebrating. On with Lou and his work …

Peter Krok
Editor-in-Chief of the SVJ

A FEW THOUGHTS ABOUT LOU MCKEE

Eileen M. D'Angelo

I first met Lou through his words. When I started to think seriously about publishing my own work, I found that all of the literary magazines that I read were publishing his poems. He was everywhere. The more I read, the more I adored his poetry. I couldn't get enough of it. Most poets have issues with consistency. We may write good poems that we believe work well, but we also write our fair share of mediocre poems that continue to cry out for editing and some that never see the light of day. To quote Emily Dickinson, there wasn't a poem that Lou wrote that didn't blow off the top of my head.

My two first meetings with Lou were memorable. Sometime in the 80's, Lou was reading at West Chester University and I went there to hear him read and get all of my books autographed. I was in my 20's, which is to say, *young.* After the reading, I ran up to Lou like a groupie at a Springsteen concert. I blurted out something to the effect of: *"a perfect night is lighting a few candles, unwinding with a glass of wine in a hot bubble bath – and reading your poems."* Within a few days, I got a copy of "The Reason I Write" in the mail and a 30 year friendship was born. Afterward, a handful of friends were organizing the Mad Poets Festival, which was then called the Food for Thought Festival. We wrote letters to some of the coolest poets in Philadelphia, and of course, we invited Lou. In our invitations, we asked for bio information and asked if the poet had needed handicapped accessibility or special accommodations. Lou took that opportunity to show us we were taking it all too seriously. When we got his RSVP back in the mail, among his other humorous rock star style demands, he asked for a jar of green M&Ms like Van Halen when they were on tour. Needless to say, I made sure I bought bags and bags of M&Ms, sorted the green ones and filled a candy jar to present to him.

I love that Lou told people he was born on St. Patrick's Day, even though he was born in dead summer on the last day of July— no where near his favorite saint's feast day. One of his old girlfriends probably still believes it's true. Years back, we started an annual ritual, a "July Birthday Party," at which many of his friends with summer birthdays met to celebrate. It was mainly to *celebrate* Lou—but he wouldn't let you do anything just for *him*, so the ruse was created. A small circle of friends were there, annually to celebrate him. Always Steve Delia and Missy Grotz. Ray Greenblatt. Pete Krok. Mike Morell. Sometimes Harry Humes and Paul Martin. It was a ploy to drag him out of hibernation. He liked the old press photo taken by Robin Hiteshew best, I think because it showed him as gruff and gray-haired, the wild muse. It reminded me of the famous photograph of Walt Whitman. I preferred the photograph that showed him with a reserved smile, because it showed the softer side that he saved for his friends.

After those parties, and after late nights in Philly, after poetry readings, we'd end up at some watering hole in old city, at Paddy's Pub, Bennigans's or Dirty Frank's, drinking Jameson and Scarlett O'Hara's (Southern Comfort and cranberry). He always said that he wanted a plaque mounted outside Paddy's with his name on it. He told me that the best thing you can say to an Irishman after a long night of revelry and music is *Goodnight you bastard!* Always the teacher, he taught me to say that in Gaelic: *Oiche Ma'haith a bastar!* So whenever I drove him home to Frankford Avenue in the wee hours of the morning, I would turn my car around in the shopping center across the street, pull up to the light facing his house and the graveyard. He would wait on the steps for me to pull away when the light turned green. I'd yell *Goodnight you bastard* out of the car window loud enough to wake the banshee; sometimes in Gaelic, sometimes not, the two of us struck by a sense of fun and a wonderful wildness, laughing like unruly teenagers instead of two middle-aged poets.

Lou was a great letter writer. And I mean *letters,* not brief and spiritless emails, although his emails were also entertaining. His letters were like diary entries, pure poetry. Below the date on a letter, he once wrote: *Deepwater, Minnesota.* In the letter, he wrote: *"Alas, I am not writing you from scenic Deepwater, Minnesota. Actually, I'm not even sure if there is a town called Deepwater in Minnesota, or even if there is deep water in Minnesota– I'm just tired of writing Philadelphia, Pennsylvania, on my letters."* AND *"Dear Eibhlin: No, it's not a secret pen name but now that I've got you toasting and cursing me in Irish, I might as well address you in the old tongue."* AND *"Dear Eileen: You end your last letter by promising you won't be as depressing in your next letter. Be whatever way you are. I like the real you—not the pleasant-always- smiling-face. Besides, it's too late to scare me away. In fact, at this point, it will probably take a court order."* And he would end his letters with great lines, too: *"Write back. It's lonely in the garret."* and *Thanks for being on the same road as I am, at the same time."*

One of the things that I miss is how we inspired each other in our writing. Once I sent him a poem about being on a dock, the wind whipping my skirt to my legs and how I couldn't tell the sea from the sky at the gray-blue horizon. He sent me *A Morning's Work.* It was the same scene, the same story, from a different and fresh perspective, as if he was there, watching from the beach. I can point to many of my poems that he inspired. Lou hated Winter— the long dark months, how the cold gets under your skin. At one point, I ended a letter by telling him Spring was coming. I said I knew because took a walk and noticed the crocuses were blooming and the ice was melting. Within days, I received *The First*

Word of Spring, which begins: *"She tells me the ice is melting..."* Our game continued for years. Of course, with many his poems, he would begin with a story that was basically true; and then, around line 6 or 7, his poem would take an erotic left turn, somewhere between truth, imagination and absolute fantasy. Maybe I should have been offended by it, but it often made me laugh. An incorrigible flirt, he only ever saw my "good side." I wrote him back once and told him that he didn't really know me, that I'm really "high maintenance," and *I'm the reason* they call my husband, "St. Frank." Soon after, I got the poem *"She Said"* in the mail.

It was a perpetual volley of words. Poems bounced back and forth. I wondered what the next envelope would bring, like a message in a bottle washing up on shore. I wondered where he would be standing in the poem I just sent to him, to show me a different viewpoint. He turned my words on their edge and created art out of the stories and poems I shared with him, literally turning my life into poetry. There was a mutual stirring of the muse I know I'll never see again. It was magical, knowing that I could be kindling for his fire, for his creative process, and he was kindling for mine. He spoke simply and eloquently, capturing his readers' emotions and experiences, as he wrote about his own. He spoke universally to everyone, for everyone. Lou had a way of drawing you into his world with his poems. His words were our words, his struggles—our struggles. He had an honesty in poems that is rarely seen and there was romance in his stories, along with a sense of longing and nostalgia. And his words— full of tenderness and sensuality – designed to help us remember the magic, the seemingly ordinary moments we take for granted. He had a gift for reaching in and touching your soul.

There is an ache inside that emerges from time to time when I think of his passing. Five years this November 21st, and it's so hard to believe that so much time has passed.

The one gift has been getting to know Michele McKee Hocker, his sweet sister, who is like my recently-discovered little sister.

Lou died too young. His poems live on, continuing to inspire. He had a dedication to the written word that I have never seen before– or since. It haunts me to think of the hundreds of poems that he will never write. So many beautiful words lost. The world is so much less, and our lives are so much less, without his true and loving heart, his colorful personality and his strong voice. *Lou, thanks for being on the same road as I was— at the same time.*

THE TRIGGERING POET:
HUGO, MCKEE & ME

I think everyone must have known him who went to Philly's
"Open Mouth" poetry series in the early '80s. We first met at
an "Open Mouth" reading hosted by Sedenger's Book Store
in Huntingdon Valley. Not a great day for a reading, rain fell
all afternoon, but a bunch of us were there to try out poems
on a small, enthusiastic audience, and our bartender for that
afternoon was one Louis McKee.

Standing in a backroom with the door open he'd peek out
and listen to readers from time to time. I grabbed a beer, put
a buck in his tip cup, and we started to talk about poetry. We
mentioned a few poets we admired until finally Dick Hugo's
name came up, and we became friends that day. Lou's
favorite Hugo poem "Degrees of Gray in Philipsburg" was
also mine. We went on to discuss Hugo's book of quirky
essays, *The Triggering Town*. We were moved by Hugo's
hubris, humor, and heart-felt humanity in those pieces. He
gave new writers license to explore ideas and perceptions
without being overly concerned about limited experience in
the world. Hugo's assertion that *You owe reality nothing and
the truth about your feelings everything* could've been our
mantra.

Lou might've told me about Hugo's forthcoming collected
poems, *Making Certain It Goes On* and of his plans to write a
review when it was published. I do remember he told me that
Hugo had once phoned to check on him when he was
suffering from some health issues. He was proud of that, and
I was impressed that Hugo would think enough of Lou to
check on his condition.

After that day, I'd see Lou in bars, bookstores, libraries and
we'd always chat about our latest literary adventures.

Gradually, however, we lost track of each other. I'd occasionally come across some of his fine poems in *American Poetry Review*, but I became preoccupied with earning a MLS in Library Science. I don't know if Lou ever published a review of Hugo's collected poems, but I have a copy of *Making Certain It Goes On*, as well as *The Triggering Town*, in the library where I work. Hugo was always our triggering poet, and I've ordered Lou's books of poetry for our shelves as well. It's my own small gesture for Lou—making certain it goes on for him, too.

~Alfred Encarnacion

When I think about Lou McKee, the first word that comes to mind is "large." Not just his physical body, but his huge heart; I don't think I've ever met anyone more large-hearted than Lou. I live in the Lehigh Valley; Lou lived in Philadelphia, so we didn't see each other a lot. In the early years, he used to come up our way to do readings at Godfrey Daniels in Bethlehem and DeSales University in Center Valley, and these were always memorable events. But then the years intervened, and travel became difficult for him, so our friendship was reduced to the occasional letter (you know, those things with stamps?), then email. I was always so happy to see his name pop up in my inbox. He was also very kind to me, using an omnibus review of my chapbooks in *One Trick Pony* and not only taking a poem for *Pony*, but also nominating it for a Pushcart Prize. It's one of those funny things of the modern world, that although my mind understands that he's gone, my heart still thinks, "Hey, I know he's a busy guy. There'll be another email coming from him, wait and see."

Among my best memories of Lou was his memorial reading, organized by Eileen D'Angelo, in Media. She'd asked us to each either read one of Lou's poems or tell an anecdote or two, and she interspersed the invited readers with open readings from the audience. The place was packed, and it was made livelier by the open bottles of Jameson's that graced the rooms. His family piled the tables with his books and chapbooks, encouraging everyone to take a book or two home with them, and I thought, "What a lovely gesture, and what better tribute?" And then the magical afternoon, listening to his words, everyone reading their favorites. I think of Lou every time I have a wee dram of whisky, and I never add any water, because I can hear Lou saying, "There's water enough in it already."

~Barbara Crooker

TRIBUTE FOR LOUIS McKEE

I don't know how many times I've taught the poems of Louis McKee in my creative writing classes, but the number is considerable, and very often, even with the most unsophisticated readers of poetry—yes, even with those students taking the course solely for what they think is an easy three credits—the poems work to effect a realization of what poetry can be, and the mindset changes; if not a satori experience, then at least a recognition that poetry is an art form that matters, that adds something to one's experience of the world. "Starting Over," the best of all the Barbie Doll poems ever written, "That Goddamn Moon," one of the most beautiful love poems in the English language, and "For the Beautiful Woman Across the Room" all have an affective impact on students, and of course McKee's poems resonate even more and on so many different levels with knowledgeable and practiced readers. McKee's poems define the best that poetry can be, so touchingly human, so deeply ensconced in what it means to be alive, that the reader is drawn back into McKee's world, often and then again, as a reminder of our need to escape the mundane world of petty politics and trivial concerns, what denotes a life of "quiet desperation" as Thoreau described it.

Apart from his consummate skill as a poet he was also a commanding editor of the journal One Trick Pony, and an acceptance there meant something because he expected poets to work on their art the same way he did, refining a poem, perfecting it, making it as good as it could be, not settling for something almost there or of the middling quality that passes in so many other publications. So an acceptance meant that you were valued as a writer, and that accolade was worth everything. He talked often about the trip to the mailbox where he unfailingly found a pile of weak submissions, and then there was the joy at finding something of value, something that reached deep, that "took the top of your head off" as Dickinson described the effect poetry should have on the reader, thus validating the mission, celebrating the beautiful virtue of poetry. He would unfailingly tell writers how much he liked their work, such generosity unusual in the intensely competitive world of creative writing. That generosity of spirit evidenced in his own poetry and in his remarkable editing sensibility reflect the best that American poetry has to offer: his voice, as is the case with the best of our literary voices, will be impossible to replicate.

Dale E. Ritterbusch
Professor of English
Department of Languages & Literatures
University of Wisconsin-Whitewater
ritterbd@uww.edu

LOUIS MCKEE, A MEMORY

I spoke with Louis McKee a few times, mostly at Mad Poets Society events. Those brief conversations along with reading some of his writing convinced me to attend his one-day workshop at the Delaware County Institute of Science in April, 2006. McKee's poetry is plain-spoken but ever surprising and revealing. His teaching that early spring morning and afternoon were the same way. There were perhaps ten of us who attended the workshop. McKee was like a good pediatrician with our poems – gentle with their handling but direct and incisive with his diagnoses of what ailed them. I kept his notes on the two poems I submitted to the workshop and recently read them again.

There were more positive comments on the pages than I expected to see, along with very specific criticisms which I'd heeded. The more problematic of my poems dealt with the ongoing horror of children forced to be soldiers. 2006 was a time when American forces were mired in two seemingly endless wars in Iraq and Afghanistan. I had struggled with how to confront the topic of violent conflict and express my disgust. McKee clearly identified the poem's deficiencies. I rewrote it, especially the last stanza, and re-titled it. Both of the poems, which benefitted from his analysis, were subsequently published.

Discussion during the workshop was lively – stimulated and guided by a generous teacher who kept the focus on our work and not himself. The combination of mastery and humility, evident in McKee's teaching, is present throughout his many books of poems. He leaves a legacy not only of his own words but of the uncountable students and colleagues whom he inspired to reach, always, for excellence.

~David P. Kozinski

MEMORIES OF LOUIS MCKEE

History: In 2001, Louis McKee's chap *Loose Change* spun out into the world, the result of Lou's insistence that I start publishing books. Marsh River Editions was born.

* Lou McKee, the reader/dreamer/poet who taught full time, who became a publisher, book collector, mentor, and email correspondent with poets

* Lou McKee, the poet who began submitting poetry to my Wisconsin poetry journal, *Free Verse*, in 2000

* Lou McKee with Guinness, the poet my husband and I happily met in Philadelphia in September 2001, weeks after 9/11

* Lou McKee, the poet who told me his *One Trick Pony* was one hundred times more significant than my *Free Verse*

* Lou McKee, the poet who wrote: *After birth, you start to die—it's all downhill*

* Lou McKee, the poet who wrote to me about poets, poetry, editing, his health, how his day was going

* Lou McKee, the poet who commented, after I said (in jest) that our emails, after much time, were getting boring: *when I put the gun to my head, I'll make sure you know that the plot is picking up some*

* Lou McKee, the poet who had the ability to write conversational, flowing, flawless poems, quiet poems of loss, no word out of tune

* Lou McKee, the poet with the right tools and his words scattered on his desk, getting (love, poetry) *this wonderful thing to fly*

* Lou McKee, the poet who left this lonely planet too soon, who will be long-remembered and missed

~Linda Aschbrenner

MEMORIES OF LOUIS MCKEE

What memories stand out of Louis C. McKee? All of them. Lou was my friend and mentor for 33 years. Lou was the kind of guy you did not forget. My first memories of Lou were seeing him, larger than life, walking at a brisk pace the mile or so from his apartment on Axe Factory Road in Northeast Philadelphia to Father Judge High School where he taught, and tearing down a football field to tackle students during the annual faculty student football game. That was before his knee problems got out of hand. For those who met Lou later in life, it may be hard for them to realize that he once was a good athlete. He played football, basketball, baseball and rugby and was an award winning shot putter. He was a power lifter into his mid to late twenties. He was large, strong, and tough, tough enough to work for a while as a bouncer at a biker bar. Later in life, on the occasions that I took my son with me to visit Lou, my son would ask, "Are we going to see the giant?" I would tell me son, "Yes, we're going to see the giant."

Much of what Lou did and how he lived smacks of legend. He had a stint as a ward leader and had first-hand knowledge of the grungier side of politics. He lived in a 120-year-old house, impossible to keep repaired. The house had rows of over-stuffed bookcases, floor to ceiling stacks of books, boxes full of books in his covered porch and upstairs rooms. Jazz music, NPR or a ball game was always playing in the background. He bought whiskey by the case. His work awed and inspired dozens of other writers. He seemed to know everyone in poetry... yet, five years after his death, there is little mention of him or his work in literary journals. It is time to correct this.

Joseph Farley
cynicpress@yahoo.com

THE POET AS ATHLETE (FOR LOU)

by W.D. Ehrhart

One look at him induces adjectives:
gargantuan, Brobdingnagian, humongous;
what manatees might look like
if they put on clothes. Somewhere under
all that vast expanse like open ocean
must be something solid, but no imagination
could be vast enough to conjure even
flaccid muscles, bones like coral atolls
in that briny, rolling sea.

Against the tide of gravity, he struggles
to the podium like someone swimming,
takes a drink of water, and begins:
a poem about the powerful intoxication
of his first car, a poem about
the expectation of a first teenaged love,
a poem about a son he doesn't have.

Surely he must know what we are thinking.
Surely he must swim through every day
against a tide of gravity and ridicule,
but in a sure voice steady as the tides,
he draws us to the heart
of what we share.

Not one word about his own affliction.
Consider poetry, how good poems
offer us the world with eyes renewed.
Now see the swimmer I am watching:
all discipline, all muscle, lean and hard.

THE ART OF LOUIS McKEE

by Philip Dacey

Classical artists inevitably run the risk of seeing their work undervalued. Given Quintilian's "The perfection of art is to conceal art" and Ovid's pithier "It is art to conceal art," the artist who follows their lead will lack the showy literary gestures some readers consider a sign of strong writing. In the dance world, virtuosity is distrusted; in the literary world, it is not distrusted enough. Lou McKee is one of those artists who eschew flash and glitter, and exploring the nature of his artistry provides a lesson in the essential humility and genius of the classical poet.

The career during which he has consistently practiced such a demanding kind of art spans many books and chapbooks, including particularly *River Architecture* (1999), a selection of much of his best work from his earlier years, and more recently *Near Occasions of Sin* (2006). Poems referred to in this appreciation can be found in either of those books or in the selection appearing elsewhere in this issue. (Editor's Note: this essay originally appeared in a previous version of the *Schuylkill Valley Journal* alongside a different selection of Lou McKee's poetry.)

One of the latter group, "Light," provides an excellent launchpad for a look at McKee's work because its relative briefness is inversely proportional to its abundant artistry.

In music, minimalism equals minimal means/maximum effect, a little developed into a lot. Similarly, "Light" is like a resonating chamber where its limited number of elements recur and vary and echo back and forth, often inconspicuously. The main element is identified in the title and recurs in numerous forms: electric lights in houses, the light of awareness ("He knew...I didn't"), a house on fire, the tip of a lit cigarette, darkness as the inverse of light. In context, "In the dark" is both literal and metaphorical, suggesting the son's insufficient understanding of his father. Also, the father darkens the house in a positive way by not wasting light whereas the now-adult son's dark carries regret, a sense of loss or waste.

Note numerous other quietly operative felicities that give this poem weight and direction: "leave" at the start refers to the allowing of lights to burn but later returns implicitly in "ran from the house" as a permanent leave-taking from the family; the father "owed" money but the son "was indebted" emotionally; "I was not coming back" broadens from its first meaning here--not returning to a room--to not ever coming home again; the father in effect ultimately "leaves" by dying but then comes back at the end, visible across the dark room. And "as though it were on fire" is poignantly ironic, given the son's departure from the house his father darkens and the son had carelessly kept lit. The implication is that what drove the son from the house was the son himself. (It ought to be said that this poem looks back to, and is in a class with, Robert Hayden's "Those Sunday Mornings." The independent strength of "Light" gives the lie to amateur poets' fear of reading lest they be influenced unduly.)

"Light," in summary, exploits its few elements to a fullness without straining or self-display. A reader can be forgiven for finding it moving while not also consciously observing and crediting its workings. The poem's dense, intricate, inventive weave of its parts is there to serve, not be the focus of attention. The poem is classically classical.

While shunning look-at-me literary performances, the Romans also loved to uncork long sentences, often periodic; i.e., grammatically unresolved until the very end. How justify them? Such sentences less advertised the poet than gave emphasis and drive to the content of them, raising the emotional ante, suggesting a state of intense and directed energy. And such sentences can be found throughout McKee's work, where they seem effortless, because of their flow.

"1962" (a good example of the historical dimension of his latest book) is 24 lines long and contains only two sentences, the second 18 lines long itself. In "Alone, Not Lonely," he unwinds a 21-line doozy of a sentence. These sentences and others like them seem to grow out of themselves, organically, not be the product of artistic manipulation; in fact, however, they're about as natural as a ballet dancer spinning repeatedly on the axis of one toe. To write in that manner, one must be less a blossoming flower than a commanding general.

"Sisyphus," while exemplifying many virtues characteristic of McKee, also demonstrates the emotional power of the long McKee sentence we've been talking about. Beginning with the word "Today," halfway through the poem, McKee gives the reader a ride--"like ice riding its own melting," as Frost said--that is syntactically the equivalent of the ride the speaker, who is in love with another man's wife, is giving to his own heart. The sentence descends the page like the Sisyphean rock itself. In the context of the poem, the non-stop sentence/descent also echoes both an extended riff by Thelonius Monk and the spinning of a quarter on a bar. Such seamless layeredness marks high artistry. (For more seamless layeredness, see "Seascape" and how it moves with such easy --i.e., hard-won--grace between ocean waves and a woman and time's give-and-take.)

"Sisyphus" allows us to segue to other strengths of McKee. I love the moment in the poem when the speaker asks, "Did I say my wife?" The question draws for us a bright, shining line between the voice we hear and the craftsman silently hammering the poem together, a line readers can easily and understandably fail to see. If the poet had really misspoke, all he'd have to do is change his wording. Instead, the "wrong word" precisely reveals the pathos and quandary of the star-crossed lover. (Wallace Stevens: "Personally, I like words to sound wrong.")

And when the lover refers to "another psychiatrist," McKee leaves out the name of Freud, not only honoring the intelligence of his readership but also acknowledging that what is unsaid sometimes communicates more than what is said. Much of a typical McKee poem, in fact, takes place in the margins or between the lines. In "Summer Neighbors," for example, about a failed human connection, he refers to the ocean's changing appearance from night to day, as it goes "black then blue, black, blue." A lesser poet would have drawn an explicit connection between emotional pain and the black-and-blue of a bruise; McKee's poem is the more powerful for his not doing so, as serious pain is beyond words. It's his reticence that speaks, if you will, of that pain.

Likewise, in "Empathy," the speaker admits, "I don't know / what to say about the events in New York City." Such a naked admission in the face of 9-11 is rare in general and almost unprecedented in poems about the tragic day. This admission is similar to "Did I say wife?" but as that one communicated pathos this one smoothly disarms the reader; we feel ourselves in the presence of honesty and vulnerability and open ourselves up to it. The poet has us where he wants us. Finally, a disarmingly casual remark, "Frank, I wish you had / been with me today" (from "Diction") leads not to an off-hand anecdote or reminiscence but to a virtual meditation on language and friendship and erotic pleasure; the deliberate tonal misdirection prevents our resistance to entertaining some hefty considerations.

The Irish poet Brendan Kennelly has called McKee "a moving, complex love-poet, at once passionate and reserved." I agree completely, and the judgment points us toward one place where McKee brings his artistry of restraint consistently to bear. After all, one of the Latin poets quoted at the start is one of the world's great love poets. Connecting the dots of classical art and love suggests that great love poems selflessly focus on the love-object or the lovers' relationship, not on displays of the writer's skills. The following line by McKee--a declaration as strikingly authoritative and personal as anything in Akhmatova--"The differences / between what two people thought / and what they said is a wildfire," is a prime example of the passionate reserve Kennelly admires.

The references to Ovid and Akhmatova remind us that McKee studied Latin (as well as Spanish) for several years and was a Russian language minor in college. And, inspired by an Auden essay, he delved further into English in a way not enough American poets have: "I eventually got one of those two-volume OED's, boxed with a magnifying glass, and for many years used it regularly." Such studiousness sets into sharp relief the artistry that hides itself but is founded upon years of preparation and the assiduous development of an aesthetic consciousness. Just as athletes train, McKee trained. (As a high-schooler, he memorized Poe's "The Bells" and won a bet; more training.)

McKee's most recent book features much attention to love. "Trespassing" economically anatomizes a triangle and ends, "The breach in the fence was not / of my doing, even if the crossing over was; / let him tend, then, to his tasks / for both--for all--our sakes." The erotic also finds a home here. The title of "Rosato" refers to both the wine and the reddened face of the woman, whose private parts are explored in public by her partner. And "In Medias Res" (not a surprising title for a classical poet) combines both a triangle and the explicit description of a sexual act.

Another, different triangle appears in "The Nurturing," where, with great tact, McKee tells the story of an adult male relieving the pressure in his best friend's nursing wife's breasts by sucking on them with the approval of the husband. And such signature tact occurs in "Starting Over," about a Barbie doll he finds and keeps as a kind of companion: in other hands the poem could have been just cute or embarrassingly lugubrious but it's pitched by McKee straightforwardly, coolly, and is all the more poignant for his doing so.

Reading these and other McKee's love poems, which often are elegiac, I thought of Wilfred Owen's "the poetry is in the pity" because pathos (pain, desire) is so prominent in so many of the poems, but it's pathos shaped and delivered by his keen ear and command of language and form. McKee knows how to negotiate between manner and matter. He speaks, as lover, of "pieces of myself I was going to give" to his beloved, but the poems are equally pieces of himself he's giving to us, his readers.

If part of McKee's art is his ability to disarm his readers and put them at ease in his presence, so that he can work his magic, one further element in his work responsible for that ability could be his Roman Catholicism. "I was waylaid on my way to the seminary -- her name was Marie McGrath, God love her," McKee has said. The term "confessionalism," used in a literary context, usually recalls Sylvia Plath and Co., but the term when applied to McKee can mean the practice of treating his readers like father-confessors and revealing to them weaknesses or failures that he has faced by means of a veritable examination of conscience. In "Rain," a poem knitted unobtrusively together by the imagery of stones, the speaker confesses he has "lusted / after the Winochek girl" and made things worse by persecuting a classmate who had done the same thing. (It's appropriate here to recall the title of McKee's latest collection, *The Near Occasions of Sin*, a book, according to Brendan Kennelly, "in the state of grace.") The effect of such confessionalism is to expose the speaker's vulnerability, to put the reader in a position that invites understanding and empathy, even forgiveness.

McKee's Irishness also pervades his work and may in part account for much of his music and rhetoric (e.g., his management of sentences). As he says in "Noblesse Oblige," he grew up with "wordslingers" in his blood. He has described his own family as "crude, rowdy, and vulgar," and is proud when a cousin, seeing McKee's blood after a minor accident, calls it "the blood of Irish kings." In the space and tension between vulgarity and royalty, the drama of McKee's poetry plays itself out. McKee's restraint as a poet is remarkable enough, but verbal restraint for an Irishman is akin to a miracle.

The very non-Irish/non-Catholic African-American blues plays its role, too, in McKee's verbal music. The blues, he tells, "has to be said / twice if anyone is going / to hear." The remarkable poem "The Angels" employs repetition so deftly it creates fugal effect. A handful of words and phrases recur and weave in and out and around each other in staggered succession. The poem as a kind of sonic tour-de-force, obsessively repetitive like John Adams or Philip Glass--there's that minimalism again--while at the same time never losing touch with the voice of the speaker recalling his adolescence. Brendan Kennelly reaffirms that combination when he says that McKee's poems have "the candour of a next-door neighbor" but also "sound like songs--winged, humane, vulnerable."

Sometimes McKee's humaneness comes across as not so much in the Western classical tradition as in the Eastern classical tradition, when he sounds fairly Chinese: "I wish you were here / sitting beside me on the riverbank." He could be Li Po missing and writing to Tu Fu.

In "Following Tracks," from *River Architecture*, McKee writes of "stones...glowing with moonlight" that "lend some hope to this miserable night." Such writing, so freighted with pathos and balanced in articulation and emotion, reminds me of Eliot on Tennyson. The modern Anglican argued that the quality of Tennyson's faith was measurable by the quality of his doubt. In McKee, the quality of his hope is measurable by the quality of his lamentations.

It is the essence of McKee's work to be rich in artifice and craftsmanship and informed poetic strategies while at the same time consistently brave in its presentation of two confrontations: a person's with himself and that person's with the world outside himself. To read McKee is to witness drama and struggle; if the art is hard-won, the human victories are, too. McKee is a bracing and welcome poet, whose artistry and accomplishment must not go unsung.

THE DEAL

by Lou McKee

If I remember correctly from my days in law school, or was it something I heard in film about a law school, there is such a thing as a "contract implied." For example, when a person invests his time, money, and energy in a project that furthers the interests of other parties, those other parties can be expected to – bound perhaps by honor if not the law – to help support the efforts being made in the furtherance of their interest. Okay, it maybe came from the movies or television, or maybe just from "formal" training in the law beyond a few seasons of *The Paper Chase* many years ago, and a messy but pretty much hands-off divorce that dates around the same time. What I know is this: I've spent a great deal of the last thirty-five years publishing books and magazines – never including my own writing, but only getting out the good work I've been lucky enough to find in others. I also know that I've had little support. I never asked for government of philanthropically-minded people to help out. I had hoped that the poets I knew, including those I published, would buy copies, subscribe, maybe even offer an occasional gift. And this did happen, but rarely. Most of the time I was shorting credit card payments to my buddies at Bank of America or Citibank, anteing up at the start of each new issue with hard-won schoolteacher dollars.

Perhaps there never was a deal. Well, there should have been. I think of all the magazines I have enjoyed over the years, from mimeo to Xerox – the ones which were built on clouds with substandard concrete mixes – which lasted a couple, a few, a dozen issues, until the noble spirits behind them, hunched over, their shoulders snug to the wheel, could not take it anymore. As I edited and published my efforts – *The Carousel Quarterly, The Axe Factory, The Painted Bride*

Quarterly, One Trick Pony, Banshee Press – I sent exchange copies to the editors I thought were doing good work elsewhere. This "in kind" trade was actually not much help in lifting the burdens from their backs, I know. They would rather have had me send a check, something that might not do much to satisfy the printers, but which could go toward the beer, another unavoidable cost when putting an issue together. Before I joined the ranks of the publishing trade, before I entered into the soul-trading pacts with the aforementioned banks, I used to keep a list of the litmags I saw or heard of that piqued my interest, and every two weeks, on pay day, I would send for another subscription. Poetry Tax, some friends and I would call it. At year's end, twenty-six subscriptions! The number seems like such a pathetic joke – checks going out each month for five or ten dollar subscriptions ... but the pleasure of finding poetry in my mailbox expectedly, but still fairly often, couldn't be beaten. If I thought an editor somewhere was doing a great job, I renewed. Sometimes, though, I jumped ships, went looking to see what else was going on. This was on top of the other habit I tried to keep going, of subscribing, as well to any magazine that had the sweet decency to accept my work. A quid pro quo, the least I could do, I thought. Besides it was not an issue all that often.

Like all good habits, this one went the way of Sister Donna Maureen's – who I heard not long ago had two grown children of her own now. I became a junkie, and started shooting my money directly into the typesetters' and printers' and post office's money boxes. Naïve, I thought I would get by on "the kindness of strangers," but it was never enough. I tell you this now as a recovering addict. I cannot say that I am done with that life completely. I don't go to the meetings – oh, I know I should. And I'm not sure I can count on my sponsor. He is a bit shaky, too, at times. You know what they say though: One day at a time.

As for the rest of you: I get it, man. And good luck to you. Ennabler that I am, I will throw a few dollars your way whenever I can and I will pay entry fees – I mean, I am trusting you, friend. We all are. Pick the good manuscripts, get the good poetry into the hands of those who will appreciate it, get the names of the good poets into the conversations of those who talk about such things. Hang in as long as you can. This is the deal, right – contract be damned! Swear on your grandmother's grave.

CHARLIE: WASN'T THAT A TIME?

by Louis McKee

I recall the spring of 1972; a poet visited the LaSalle College campus to read his poems. I had never heard of C. K. Williams, but at that point I had heard of very few poets. At an early age I became enamored of words, and found Long-fellow and Whittier, Frost and Kilmer, in the books I saw. In high school I met up with Keats, Shelley, and Byron, with Wordsworth and Yeats. It was during that time that I became obsessed with the Beats. I went to see Ginsburg – see, I think, more than hear – read as part of a troupe of Poets Against the Vietnam War, and as a result I saw and heard Bly, Kinnell, Logan, Levertov, Wright, and others. Thinking back on it, I had come honestly upon a decent foundation, but still much was new to me with every passing day, with each class, each book and magazine, each conversation in the snack bar of the College Union.

One day in March, 1972, in the theater of the College Union, C. K. Williams read poems that made an impression on me. I sought out his books, *Lies*, and *I am the Bitter Name*. I even found copies of a small single-poem booklet, *A Day for Anne Frank*, selling for a dollar each at Middle Earth Books, a wonderful small shop on Pine Street. I bought five copies, and shared them with my friends at school who were equally smitten with the poet's work.

A couple of years later I was graduated, in grad school at night, and teaching high school English. My friends from LaSalle, fellow would-be poets, serious writers all of them, and seemingly committed to the game, had scattered, to schools, jobs, relationships – what we laughingly, bitterly, in reflection, called life. Things were okay, but not like they had been.

I saw a notice, not much bigger than a classified ad, in glossy *Philadelphia Magazine*, announcing a Poetry Workshop that was being offered at the Jewish Y on Pine Street. I missed the annual spring workshops and creative writing classes of college, and the rigor and tedium of grad school was beating me up. I though a workshop might relax some of the muscles in my body and mind which were pinched much too tight. The workshop would be led by C. K. Williams.

I remember little about the first meeting, except for the crowd. Believe it or not – and I was amazed too – it was a crowd. Young and old and in between, and, as I would find out eventually, ranging from novice to wonderfully skilled. And C. K. Williams, tall, quiet – I often wondered what he thought of that turn-out – in the middle of the throng.

There were so many in the room that night that very little could be accomplished. It was decided, though, that there would be two groups, one meeting Tuesdays, and the other Thursdays, and so we were divided, before we all got to sit in a circle, say hello and read one of our poems aloud.

The next week, when I showed up on my designated night, I was one of about eighteen; apparently a handful had had second thoughts. This attrition would continue, in both groups, until a couple of weeks along Charlie, as we now called him, suggested that we roll into one, and back to one night. The crowd was now down to a couple of handfuls, but the diversity was still there, and the range of skills.

Charlie was good – smart and perceptive, insightful, and very much together; he handled the sessions well, a couple of hours a night, allowing everyone their say, encouraging everyone to get involved. But he was tough, too -- he could reach inside a poem he only just saw for the first time, and like a surgeon in a comedy skit pull this and that out, move that thing over to there, and that one, just a slight nudge.

Of course, there were some who broke the cardinal rule of poetry workshops; they brought in work that, to their minds, was finished, done – perfect. Some brought poems to which they were too emotionally attached. It hurts to have your work discussed critically, objectively, honestly. With Charlie setting the tone, and some smart, capable people in the group, that's what would happen. Along with attrition.

That workshop went through a number of versions. Originally, I think, to run ten weeks, a semester, it went on for four, maybe five, semesters. Twelve to sixteen people would start each term, a few new faces joining the hard core, with a couple new and old faces dropping out here and there.

Actually, the workshops at the Y went on for years – after Charlie gave it up, I recall Richard O'Connell, Stephen Berg and Sonia Sanchez, among others, taking it on. "Charlie's group" gave way to other, newer, younger (?) poets. For all I know, it may still be going strong. But those times, with C. K. Williams at the head of the table, were special.

I remember Margaret Levinson; she struck me the first time I saw her, at that cattle call of poets; much older than the rest of us, frail looking but feisty, with her wonderful poet's hat. She was our Marianne Moore. Susan Stewart, now a Chancellor of that revolving Olympus of the Academy of American Poets, (where she sits at the table again with C. K. Williams,) was part of the group. As were Jeanne Murray Walker, Elaine Terranova, Deborah Burnham, Sandra Kohler, Betsy Fogelman, Darcy Cummings, Amy Small, and Bickley Rivera. This was the core, the faces around the table.

And C. K. Williams, who during this time, it turned out, was rolling around those new long-winding narrative meditations with their lengthy, breathy lines that would be showing up later in *With Ignorance* and *Tar*.

What a great way to spend my Tuesday nights.

So, what brought on this flashback? C. K. Williams is reading tonight, as I am writing this, in Philadelphia, a rare return visit, from his new collection of poems, *Wait*. Unable to attend the reading, and impressed by the new poems, I thought I might write Charlie a note, touch base, say hi, congratulate him on another good book, another good impression he has made on me. Ever the mentor.

Then I thought, rather than intrude on him, why not just write a review of the book. I like the poems a lot, actually think that this is his best collection in a long time, better than *The Singing*, which won the National Book Award for 2003, and maybe even better than *Repair*, for which he received the Pulitzer Prize in 1999.

Then I started thinking, remembering. And here I am, more than a thousand words into something, but it is hardly a review. I've only just mentioned *Wait* (Farrar, Straus, Giroux, $25,) and though I said the poems are good, I have not mentioned the creatures and critters he writes about: the apes he came to dislike after witnessing their violent abhorrent behavior; the sad thrush fledgling, physically deformed from birth, who will be abandoned soon by its mother; the rats who are driven to the fields and streets by a long drought; the wasp beating its head silly against a window pane; the basset hound who, like the poet, has apparently taking an interest in a particularly good looking woman; an insect he can't identify moving in circles around a formica tabletop: "It can't even trace a straight line, / but it circumnavigates the table. / Doesn't it know it's back where it began?"

I've not said anything about the German POWs he saw as a child behind the barbed wire of a prison camp; or the consideration of shrapnel; or the lies politicians tell; or the crowded loneliness of Coleridge; or the assumptions made to create religion.

My personal favorites, initially, though I know I'll change my mind again and again, include his account of visiting to the Delaware River where the vast *S. S. United States* is docked, socked in mothballs, awaiting its fate, the very ship he set sail on "the first time I ran away to France;"

That such a monster could be lifted by mere waves
and in the storm that hit us halfway across
tossed left and right until we vomited
seemed a violation of some natural law.

At Le Havre we were out of scale with everything;
when a swarm of tiny tugs nudged like piglets
at the teat, the towering mass of us in place,
all the continent of Europe looked small.

Then there is his vision of Martin Luther King's return, and the world he finds, forty years after his murder; and especially, his memory of seeing, as a boy, the Great Blackstone saw a woman in half, and "make doves and then a horse before our eyes vanish."

he used a gigantic buzz saw, and the woman let out a shriek
        that out-shrieked
the whirling blade and drilled directly into the void of our
        little boy crotches.

While the poetry community can wrestle with the facts and the metaphors in search of the kind of truths that they have come to expect from the poems of C. K. Williams, and they marvel at the crisp and terse imagery, the crackling colloquial language, there are a few of us who will be drawn back to a corner room on the second floor of the Jewish Y at Broad and Pine with its long paper-covered table, heavy chairs, and old dark windows. Speaking for myself, I learned a lot in that room, about poetry and about life. I've told people for years that you will not find the fingerprints of Charlie Williams on anything I write, but don't for a minute think that his voice, his breath, are not hanging around in any room my poems and I are ever in together.

Wait, this new book of poems by C. K. Williams, is pretty damn good; but then, I guess I'm biased.

ALONE, NOT LONELY

In a last minute to hold on
to something I could not name
I picked a wildflower from a field
in Knoxville that was mostly weeds
and dirt and broken glass where we walked,
a woman and I, who had become friends
quickly that afternoon over bottles of beer
in a dirty, harshly lit bar that should have
been a luncheonette, thought if it were
you would not have eaten there. Anyway,
the woman and I had gone for a walk
through the back door and into an open field
where she seemed to think it was safe
to share a joint, though I'm not so sure
that was what I was after - as if it were
a purple flower I was looking for
but in the end that is what I got,
and I was still holding in my hand
when my bus pulled away from the depot
across the street and I looked out
the window pretending she was there
waving goodbye with a smile bigger
than all of Tennessee instead
of back inside the dumpy bar, looking
for another stranger to buy here drinks
who might share a joint, a drink or two
and take nothing with him when he left
except maybe a flower neither of them
could name, one of those you can find
in every weedy corner of the state.
I was carrying a book for the long ride
home, but I don't remember which one.

It is somewhere on my shelves now,
and in it there is written a name and number.
In case you ever get to Knoxville again,
in case Philadelphia ever gets lonely,
and there is a flower too, an unnamed
purple weed, like one of those you'll
find in every corner of Tennessee, should you
get the chance to go looking for it.

AFTER THE SIXTH VISIT

That's the one
where you lie
back and say no-
thing, everything
having been said
at least five times
already, and she
says, well, what
are you thinking
right now? and you
tell her that
you're thinking you
want to fuck her
and she says why
do you think that
is? but it is
too late, time is
gone, fifty minute
hours, seventy
dollars, and you
know when you leave
that you won't be
back, you are better
than you have
any right to expect.

STARTING OVER

After the divorce it took awhile
in a small cheap apartment
but finally I got another house,
this one bigger, emptier.
I moved in with nothing
of my own to fill the rooms,
but still threw out the two chairs
and table the previous owners left.
I kept the doll I found
in the yard, a Barbie with matted
blond hair and not a stitch
of clothing. New wife,
I thought, and I proposed to her
right there in the middle
of my cutting the grass, lifting
my beer in a toast to love
and long years together, and though
I doubt she really wanted it,
I did pour some on her hard pretty body,
and used my finger to rub away
the mud that was caked all over her.
Later I actually bathed her
in lemon-scented Joy, along with
the dish and glass I'd used for breakfast,
lunch, and dinner.

              I didn't feel weird
about any of this yet; this was still weeks
before I was in K-Mart and bought
the outfit, jeans and plaid flannel shirt,
cowgirl Barbie, but for comfort, really,
something to wear around the house.

It would have been wrong if I'd gotten
the tight black sequined dress I saw,
or the hot baby blue mini with the silver
belt and matching fuck-me pumps.
It would have been wrong if I had
kept her naked, sitting on the bookcase
bare-assed for all the world to see.
But is this so wrong?

                    She listens to me
sometimes: sometimes I can tell.
she is not paying attention at all,
but that's okay; sometimes I'm not much
for talking myself. She is always there
when I need her though. Is that so wrong?
And I'm always there for her.

                    The yard
is her nightmare, but she knows I won't
let that happen to her again. I'm not so sure
about the life she's had, the station to which
she's been accustomed, but it is good her,
in this big empty house. She is treated well,
And her wardrobe, now, is next to none.

THE REASON I WRITE

—for Eileen

I like to think she (I like to think *she*)
has somehow worked herself loose
late on a Saturday afternoon or late evening,
chores set aside, and the family gone,
and put Miles, or maybe Monk, sweet ballads,
though, nothing hard or heady, on the stereo,
then drawn a hot bath with oil and bubbles
and a chilled bottle of Lambrusco.
I like to think she gets naked
and looks at herself in the full-length mirror;
as she does, and with a smile, slips
into the soft bliss of soapy comfort,
the almost-too-hot water uncomfortable
for just a moment but then just right.
With her wondrous hair pulled up,
she uses it as a pillow, pours a glass
of wine, then picks up a book of poems.
This is where I come in: they are my poems.
This is the reason they were written.
The rest of you, get your muses where you can.
I write for this woman, naked in a hot bath
under a modesty of bubbles. This is our
moment. Our poem. You find your own.

BIRTHDAY POEM

It's my birthday,
and she is floating naked
on the cold evening water
of her boss' pool – what
he doesn't know won't
hurt anyone, and besides
he is in the Caribbean,
so why would he care
that she is in his pool
with her husband and a girlfriend,
a few margaritas farther along
that perhaps is a good idea,
but it makes perfect sense
to her, floating
beneath a nearly full moon,
laughing in the hot tub
like children who know a joke
isn't funny, and that's exactly
what's so funny about it, and then,
standing under the shower,
turning slowly for the stars to see,
rinsing away the guilt, sobering
the celebration with soft towels.
It's my birthday
and I am alone, unable to sleep
in these hot sheets, staring at
the same old ceiling. I think
I might dream something cooler.
It's not the heat, they say,
it's the humidity. And nothing
about the ceiling tells me differently.

FIRST WORD OF SPRING

She tells me the ice
is finally melting;
I can only assume
she means the crust
along the weedy creek
banks, the crisp ply
that makes grass talk
underfoot, the glaze
and glint high in crags
of the sad stone face
over the river.
When hearts thaw,
we don't need to be
told. The melt is
tremendous; rivers
flood, and miles away,
even as far as I am,
there are fast runnels
washing with all
the gold sun they can
past my door.

LIGHT

Young, I would leave
lights on, and Father,
a few steps behind me,
would turn them off.
He knew what I didn't;
that despite my intentions,
I wasn't coming back.
He only used what light
he needed, for newspapers
and crosswords, for calculating
what he owed to whom
and why. I never knew
how much I was indebted,
and ran from the house
as though it were on fire.
Old, now, it should be
easier to sit in the dark.
Sometimes I think I see him,
my father, sitting across
the darkroom, only the red
burn of his cigarette moving.

FOLLOWING TRACKS

From a moving train, through windows
smeared with the dirty air of a dozen states,
there is nothing to be seen.
just stones, behind us and getting
farther away, glowing with moonlight.
They are irretrievable now, but still
lend some hope to this miserable night.
Ahead there is another town;
I don't know that yet, and tonight
I am quick to doubt it, but tracks
always go on to another town.
There will be more lights there,
more stones shining with the bellyful
of moon. You can trust a rain
on a miserable night, and the promise of stones.

RAIN

It is the rain: this afternoon
I had to walk home
through an unexpected storm,
and it has been coming down
steadily since. I think of Stephen
and the stones he suffered.
I think of Chet, He was slow,
the kind of boy who had trouble
writing his name, counting change
but who turned hits and at bats
in his head every night and knew
the averages of every starter
in the National League. One day
he dropped his pants
in front of Debbie Winochek
and she screamed Rape!
There is more or less
to this story; it comes through years,
and the gossip line, like pails
paused hand to hand by volunteers
at a fire. What happened here
is not important, though, not
to me. It isn't what happened
that afternoon in the Winochek's basement
that matters. It's not
what I think about tonight, listening
as I am to the rain beating like stones
on the roof. I remember Chet,
that last time I saw him – I don't know
what happened to him, what came
of the whole thing; I only recall
how a week or so later we saw him
sitting by himself on the tracks behind Sears

and how we acted as one, my friends
and I, picking up stones and throwing them
down at him, and how he was scared
and screamed and cried, but we ignored it,
angry, righteous avenging angels,
who, ourselves, each of us, had lusted
after the Winochek girl, but knew
enough not to do anything about it.

SEASCAPE

Once I stood here with some regularity
and watched the waves mount the morning,
rolling up only to come undone on the beach.
I saw monotony, the day by day
echoing of the hour. Today, time
is nearly gone, and breakers still crest
white with a start, like a woman I knew
who would tease me by flashing her breasts
when life was insisting other things
were more important. I loved her for that,
even though I knew she was doing it
because she could do no more,
and this was something she hoped
I would hold on to until, some time when
things slowed down, or stilled,
but the waves keep coming, keep dying
in the sand. If I raise my eyes though,
the white wash of another wave breaks
the blues, like a breast, a lovely promise.
They told me when I was young
to keep my back straight, my head up high –
the thing is, to keep your eye on the horizon.

TRESPASSING

Men have measured their ends
and driven stakes, laid rocks,
along the edges. Fences were built,
and it was understood, the idea,
that one has a right to his own.
Tonight I roll my fingers
through a wisp of hair loosed
at a woman's neck and linger.
I look with sadness into sad eyes –
Another man's world, I covet it.
The breach in the fence was not
of my doing, even if the crossing over was;
let him tend, then, to his tasks
for both, for all, our sakes.

ON BEING ASKED TO WRITE A POEM

Luray Gross

In China, my friend tells me, one never steps
into the shadow of one's teacher, which is to say
even on days most clouded by despair,
one must walk at a seemly distance

keeping space on each side, space before
and after – a complete circle for the moving shadow,
the teacher's searching mind and its wings.

One of my friend's own students told her this,
but she can't vouch for it in the way she is sure
that in Book Seven of the Analects of Confucius,
the sage is quoted: *If I hold up one corner,
and a man cannot come back to me with the other three,
I do not continue the lesson.*

But we have not read Confucius. We come to class,
to your crowded office, *leaning into your shadow,*
barely keeping hold of one corner, perhaps two,
each time expecting a little miracle

to make words lie down on paper like refugees
on a dusty floor, like airplanes settling on tarmac,
like newborns put to sleep on their backs
in a row of plastic cribs.

Surely Sisyphus sang to the stone as he pushed it up
the familiar slope, an intimate song sung first
for that which gave him pleasure, gave him pain.
It is what you know, what you teach:
Language will not abandon us,
will say what needs to be said, enough
to make the world a burden we can bear.

BLISS

Eileen Daly Moeller

is stitched together with pine needles and song.
The air is a clean quilt wrapped around you.
It smells like dug earth and resin.

The world is clothed in such rough bark.
Whatever softness it has is often out of reach,
until rain begins to sift through the overhanging leaves
like it could go on for at least a hundred years.

You watch small birds tumble out of the branches,
like heavy droplets, hitting the ground and rising
with a chirp, then falling again, over and over,
and you have a front row seat to their
little circus, which goes on for over an hour.

Soon you've forgotten everything else,
who you are, what you had to do today,
whether or not you are worthy of this
emptying out that comes to you, this
letting go, that allows you to enter your body,
that animal that loves you, and never tires of waiting.

THINK OF A SUMMER NIGHT

Julie Murphy

I peeled my clothes off sweaty skin,
the extra tug it took like shucking corn,
and the water opened to receive me, its dark
shimmer in starlight, and I could dive under,
the cool water sweeping my naked body,
entering every pore and the darkness
doing the same. Then I stood ankle deep
in the muddy bottom, arms stretched
over the calm surface of blackened water,
weightless, I rolled onto my back,
kicked away from shore and shadows
of trees to see the whole sky above,
the Milky Way—a thick streak.
The stars were far and close at once,
and it seemed my only purpose was to
witness them, and I did, I breathed
them into my lungs and the current's quiet
swirl braided my hair with seaweed,
my body grew cool, then cold
as I floated for hours, maybe years,
long after my skin puckered
and then the old doubts that plagued me,
that constant tick of rumination, fell away,
my mind moving toward this vast
embrace, the eons of darkness raining down
from the heavens, rising up from the earth
and the bottom of the lake.

ON THE LACE LICHEN TRAIL
SHE MOURNS A TREE AFTER A WEEK OF STORMS

Lisa Meckel

Off the trail another great pine massacred by wind
   and rain. This great gray-chested body felled,
no longer a giant against the horizon.

Its ripped-out roots cemented with dried mud
   and rocks, a fifty-fingered hand, raised
out of its element, clawing for the sky.

Who heard this tree crack, break, saw it sway
   and swing down to death?
Nothing human maimed it, only the elements,

only life circling itself. Yet here, as if in the crook of its arm
   a sticky-monkey-flower sprouts,
soon to blossom like honey from the ruins.

I too would settle into that nesty crevice, even would have waited
   with you in the storm; hunkered down on the distant grasses
heard your creak and moan. In the terror of the wind

I'd shout out love to you to lighten the death
   of your going down
and when the storms stopped I would have planted wild iris

in your earth; soothed you with the blue peace of ceanothus.
   But, sooner than any star's light reaches earth
our sun will dry your bones, rains soften your bark, creatures will

live in and off you, nest under your long trunk, until your remains
   rise up in the heat of fire or your cells dissolve
into the earth. All of this, long after my voice has given up its song.

LET US

David Adès

Let us go to a beach at night, say, on the coast of Goa,
where the moon is either a splinter of memory or anticipation
and the only spillage of light is a minimalism of stars.

Let us speak in the darkness, away from the marauding
packs of dogs and their frantic chasings, with the sound of waves
background music to our murmurings.

Let us unburden ourselves, in the way of intimates,
of the weight of accumulated baggage, of diversions
and distractions, of every unnamed fear gnawing in our hearts.

Let us shed all the skins we have taken to wearing,
all our petty concerns, the writhing worm of mortality
in our guts, our moral failings, our human shortcomings.

Let us make a bonfire of everything discarded, and show
one another the essence of what remains, vital, alive, brimming,
lightness and glow of the fire flickering on our lovely faces.

TRANSIT OF MERCURY

Helen Wickes

That little-guy planet crossing the sun today,
invisible to the, what they call, naked eye,
so you get the apparatus to keep blindness
at bay, or better still, set loose your imagining
of what's out there

      hurtling through space,
though also through human time, while you
huddle on the BART train, your fellow peeps
loud, troubled, troubling—so many of us
are outliers—then trudging home, the cop car
edging along. Space-time,

      Mr. Einstein, we're working it out,
not always well, so back to you, Brother Mercury,
you spilled and poisonous magnificence
from the broken thermometer, teasing your way
through droplets of slinky meanderings,
but then here's also to you,

      dapper little god of messages, parlaying
your all into heritage and glory, you fast dude
on the medicine labels, with your winged feet
and hat, live on, small wonder, keep it going.

UNTIL SHE SAW ME

Cobber Stumpy Malloy

Until she saw me, I was chimera,
figment, apparition, I was unseen.

She was looking for love, she said,

when I first appeared before her
like a slanted ray of morning light,

she was looking for love and then some.

Buffeted, she was looking for someone
to lean into, someone to hold,

a windbreak, an anchorman,

worry lines already on her face,
crow's feet around her eyes.

Of all possibilities, her eyes fixed on me,

seeing what everyone else had missed.
I resolved before her, solidified,

emerged from outline to substance,

from figment to form.
Arms around her I wanted to be enough,

to hold her firmly in place, secure,

but I was already too late,
the wind streaming her hair,

her eyes elsewhere, her body slender light,

her voice trembling, and she,
slipping through my hands,

lost within herself, disappearing,

leaving me standing there,
present, fully formed, alone.

EQUAL DEPENDENCE IN AN UNFORGIVING WORLD

Yvonne Higgins Leach

I.

In a row, the stable horses
repeat the history of their days:
hooves flick sand in their four-beat footfalls
the bob of head and neck like
bruised flowers in a breeze
ears back against the world
the midmorning glare of sun breaking
on their flanks as they parallel the beating coastline.

II.

Under a brimmed hat, long sleeves, and jeans
the owner pulls them to resort fronts
does not wave or call; the horse as reverence
is enough of a draw. Then
all day, up and down the beach
the tourists mount their swaybacks.
Their texture of muscles ripples.
Their damp hair smells warm when
they break sweat.
The evidence of strength in the rump
of the horse in front. An occasional
snort of exhaustion.

III.

Back at the makeshift shelter
butting another resort, sundown
the owner performs his sacred gestures
leads them to a bucket of water
lifts their saddles, sweat stains their shivering backs
like worn maps. The smooth stroke
of brush against their anatomy of back
and barrel and buttock
the drop of hay to the ground.

THE NORTHERN LIGHTS

Carla McGill

What is a circumference, but a meander
on the outside? An excursion to equivalence?
Meanwhile, the earth's core
is forced into ultimate pressure.
Even the poles have shifted
while all the world is bubbling
at the party. Creatures on the ocean
floor move toward an eruption
of something that could be
just another deficiency.
Yet moving is better than waiting
and they move with spirit.
Lions carry off the flesh and guard
the lair, knowing that substance
must be held onto in the inevitable
commotion. The surface
is full of frenzies and storms.
Grab hold of the invisible bar
that goes from the center to magnetic
north and hold on, even as things
dislodge, weeping at light speed,
and vow to remain fixed until
all the particles have dispersed,
become purple and blue
in the magnetic field. Then rejoice.

LUNAR ECLIPSE

Erik Bendix

The guardian moon
so often gapes at us
with open mouth or
turns in profile to show its
pockmarked shunning back,
yet this hour it slowly turns
to blink a bloodshot angry eye
staring into our massive shadow
as it steals hooded from its day.
We are globe-headed or
else we would not guess
its sphere could be a face,
but even skinks or fish
or swooping falcons might
conceive it was a giant eye.
Night owls and crickets
fall into deadened hush
as if at risk the light by
which we live could dim
this very last of times.
The blood hue of our
planet shadow's edge
drops its eyelid heavily
into dreams of ovulation
rounded in a cosmic womb,

a swelling of our follies
to a pregnancy that could
disgorge into darkness some
nightmare in place of answer
to our prayers: may we rise
from bleeding shadows
cast by our angry wars and
cramping clench of mind,
may the coming eyelid lift
show us that we are still alive,
reborn awake and stunned,
like night moths caught

still fluttering in the
sparkling warmth and
squinting yawns of
early morning sun.

BROWN MOTH ON WINDSHIELD

Joseph A. Chelius

Little stowaway behind the left wiper blade,
how I admired your tenacity—
your stick-to-itiveness—
as I flitted on the morning commute
from sports talk to the classical music station,
then back to sports talk after the calamity
of an Eagles' preseason defeat.

Out of the cul-de-sac we drove—
away from the common life
with its dry cleaners and pizza shop,
the deposed kingdom of the video store
still wearing the imprint of its missing sign.

By the time we reached the Turnpike,
I was reflecting on our solidarity:
me with a crick in the neck
and tension in both forearms
as we merged with the tractor trailers;
you full of wanderlust, giving new meaning
to riding shotgun—through the thrill
of buffeting wind.

As traffic slowed and the usual convoy
with Rob's Towing and State Farm Insurance
shuddered past on the shoulder,
I forgot you for a while, grew preoccupied
with deadlines, bulging job jackets,
but when we entered the corporate environs

I couldn't help wondering if you'd embrace
your new surroundings—see them as an idyll
minus cats and floating plastic bags—
or feel as disconcerted as I'd felt
on my first days
when I'd taken in all this sculpted shrubbery,
the line of trees like a welcoming committee,
standing by on their pedestals of dirt.

And all the cars in the parking lot
that had reminded me with mild dread—
or perhaps panic—
of the school yard at Most Blessed Sacrament,
the nuns with their clickers,
those perfect formations.

SWATTING AWAY BUGS

Erik Bendix

These woods have tiny humming guards
who seek out tear ducts, ear holes, even
corneal slime, anything that might
orient a sweating woodsman
to his actual whereabouts.
Abuzz, they dive and land
in suicidal ecstasy, risking
death by frenzied swat,
but rendering the glory
of their green heartland
world invisible forever.
Perhaps they sense our
ears or eyes as flowers
cupped with sweet salt
nectar brimming with
the tears of our defeat.

THAT WINTER

Hayden Saunier

I labored at life like it was a hard-edged
thing: grim, separate. All winter it snowed.

Details piled up, erased other details, the world gone
blank and full of bright cold packed to the horizon

with its scaffold of trees and stars and the scar-sound
nightly of huge plows scraping the iced roads raw.

Spikes strapped to my feet, I shoveled, chipped, kept
my eyes fixed on one narrow treacherous path

while the feathery black plume of my dog's tail
wrote epics back and forth across each bright field.

DEEP RUN

Hayden Saunier

Ice-shuttered, the creek
changes course under cover,
scratches out a new path
grain by granite grain.

I stop at the crossing,
try to enter that privacy.
This doesn't last long.

I'm restless, human.
I twist every moment
toward me.

And today is far colder
than my wish to be like a stream:
to make my way
around what's hard,
polish pebble to sand,
sharp into smooth,
be both body and bed,
particle and wave,
no matter the weather,
but even as I say it
I know I'm the stone,
not the water.
I'm always the stone.

WINTERIZED

George Drew

> "*...winter is the only time*
> *We get to walk on water.*"
> —Stuart Bartow

Frozen water, of course, but still water,
still liquid, like the right combination
of vowels and consonants, so an apt metaphor
for what I wasn't thinking about or feeling
the flow of on that day in December
when I watched the boy go down not more
than three feet away—poetry. Never had I wished
to play the role of savior more than then,
there on the shattered edge of the ice,
flat on my churning gut, the lake gurgling
under the ice from the boy's wild thrashing.
Jesus, I first thought, then said aloud,
Oh Jesus, sweet Jesus H fucking Christ...
How I wished I could rise to my feet,
step gingerly on the water's blue back
and moving heel to toes to heel ahead make it out
to the boy, free him from the icy clutch
he might have been destined to for all I knew,
and lift him, lift him tenderly toward the warm
hosannas of the sun. I could see people lined up
on the shore like skeptics wanting to watch the Ark
sink. And the Ark did, it sank, and as it did
I abandoned ship and headed back to shore.
Hurry, hurry, a voice from inside the wind hissed,
and I tried, but both coming out and going back
the best I could do was crawl, undulant on ice.

YOU KNOW WHO YOU ARE

Matt Lake

Dedicated to everyone who ever annoyed you
Like an unrepentant sadist
You turn pain into an art.
Like galloping pneumonia
You penetrate my heart.
Like Frankenstein's assistant's
No-one likes your hunch.
Like the Tilt-A-Whirl at a funfair
You make me lose my lunch.
You put the bore in boardwalk
The lid on a holiday.
The moment you walk up to me
I want to walk away.
Every cat you ever owned
Took all of its nine lives.
You give me the home of a million bees hives.
Your median hateful quotient
Graphs on exponential curves.
Like an epic case of shingles
You get on all my nerves.
People lose the will to live
Whenever you come in
Murder's not an option—
You're not worth a mortal sin.
All of us have thought this
But not said it to your face:
Your sudden disappearance
Would improve the human race.

Everyone you drive past
Or who sees you on the road
Wishes that the car you're in
Would just up and explode.
When you walk it's like the summer—
We're waiting for the Fall.
Like a nice warm bowl of mayonnaise
You nauseate us all.
You got no style
You got no rhythm
Or idea what you get to do with 'em
You got no class
No social station
And precious little conversation
Whenever people smile at you
it's not some social game;
They're privately imagining you
Bursting into flame.
Everybody here
And that includes all of the staff
Eagerly awaits the day
They'll read your epitaph.
Like the Port-o-Sans at Woodstock
I think you're full of crap
I'm glad to state you're two-faced
'Cause that gives me more to slap.
The parents that begat you
Violated nature's laws.
It would take a couple of terabytes
To catalogue your flaws.
We can't depend on magic
Or Santa's helper elf,
So vis-a-vis your getting lost:
You handle that yourself.

BLACKFLIES

Joan Colby

They descend in umbrellas of trouble.
The foxhound howls, rolling in the grass,
Her belly thick with feeding specks.

Shuddering, a man in waders
Reels in his line. The sky darkens.
He seizes his creel, the fish crawling with marauders.

It is the singular mammal that makes the news.
The bear attack. The mountain lion. But it's the pests
Small and voracious, we learn to dread.

In a marriage, it's not the definitive fight
That is to blame, but the little persistent bites
Until the back of the neck is one red welt,

Until even the eyelids swell,
The hands measled, the scourged belt
Of flesh between pantsleg and sock.

When they arrived in a blanket of woe,
You dropped the camera and ran for the truck
Swearing you'd never be back

In a season like this, how the vows you meant
On the beautiful afternoon are moot
Now that the wind has lifted them

Into the story,
Now that the trunk
Has been opened and everything loosed.

RUE DE MONTPARNASSE

Robert Brian Mulder

The girl's mother is out in front
Five steps ahead
Clenching her jellied jaw
Her dark eyes like small stones
And the girl, the poor girl
Tall, stiff, angular
Walking behind her mother
Five steps behind
Dutifully toting her cello
In its hard black case
The size of a child's coffin
Moving woodenly, with the mechanics
Of a marionette
Jerked involuntarily to life.

When I approach
Passing by the girl's mother
Whose labored breath
Whistles through cement-colored teeth
I try to catch the girl's eye
Ready with a smile tailored to say,
It will not always be as it is now—

But the girl's large, pale eyes
Are angled up and away—gazing, it seems,
Beyond the solid dome of gray sky—
Like those of a penitent in a Medieval icon
Seeking light from another world.

FROM A TRAIN WINDOW

Michele A. Belluomini

it's nearing 5pm this second of November
and the light is glowing on the trees

I watch the countryside roll away
while geese fly chevrons overhead

how to describe such light
sunset's molten copper burnishes air

unreal, real
as real, unreal my face in the train's window

now houses small and large the sere grass
become more than what they are in day's bright light

here and there house lights flicker
a hawk circles one last time before settling

tapestry of trees, fields, houses grow dimmer
sky, a delicate blue; the inside of a porcelain cup

and then, dark.

SATURDAY CHORES WITH JEHOVAH'S WITNESSES

Joseph A. Chelius

The first mild weekend, and in their dark attire
they start down the block
like something shaken from a can,
dispersing onto the row house porches,
proclaiming to the citizens of Olney
that they are free to put up their toilet brushes,
their rags and Dutch cleanser—
that world's end is at hand.
Behind parted curtains I vacillate,
as always, between listening with forbearance
and staying out of view,
sorry for the children, dragged along in their miniature suits,
yet envious of such certitude,
a glow no curt remark, no slammed door
can extinguish, the vacuum wailing
as I remember from my catechism
that envy is one of the seven deadly sins,
God with a green marker,
finding my name in the thick ledger
He keeps for venial infractions,
making His precise mark before closing the heavy cover,
dust motes swirling like purgatorial souls.

PURGE

Joseph A. Chelius

As I lay sick in bed my eyes in a restless orbit
kept turning to the United States presidents
as somber as jurors peering down from the wall—
from Washington to Lyndon Johnson
listening for the doctor to trudge
up the stairs and into the sick room
with his gleaming instruments—
cold stethoscope, probing thermometer—
in a worn black kit.

Such authority he exuded full of brusque jokes
and priestly power, scribbling on a tablet,
my mother like a dutiful parishioner
left to abide by those archaic remedies
of enemas and alcohol sponge baths—
spoon bitter medicine around the clock.

And next morning in that emptied house
to appear in her pale robe
and once more place a hand on my forehead,
remove the wadded tissues, bring ginger ale.
She'd stack the hifi downstairs
with vinyl crackling like fat on a stove—
songs from *The King & I* and *The Scottish Soldier,*
Christmas music out of season,
The Little Drummer Boy as if leading a purge,
cutting through the mist
of the humidifier, Vicks VapoRub,
softening the countenance of Millard Fillmore,
bearded Benjamin Harrison—presidents
in their imperious order,
aloof, preoccupied with national concerns
while my mother tended a boy in bed.

NEARING THE END OF APRIL

Julie Murphy

There's nothing here that hasn't happened before,
my father tells me, his voice crackling on the phone.
What he means is he is close to that other side,
the after we know nothing about.
What he means is the ordinary becomes extraordinary.
This summer, he tells me, *I'm going to spend*
more time out on the patio. I don't care
if it's another cool summer. I think it might be possible.
Nothing new about it at all. He says it again. Sighs.
I just want to go home. I just want to love your mother.
I picture him so clearly—
the thick calves, the broad back, the arms and hands
with he-man muscles. The man who built cabinets, laid bricks,
drove medics in the Philippines. Who did everything, anything,
for us. Whatever it took. Now he's happy imagining
a garden of tomato plants and cucumbers,
watching today's ballgame, eating the fresh honeydew
melon they give him for breakfast,
each day determined. When I hear him getting tired,
I want to carry him back home, like he used to carry me
from the car to the house, all those times I pretended
I was asleep and he never let on that he knew I wasn't.

THE STORY OF A COWARD

Evalyn Lee

I made the mistake
Of telling my father how much
I loved to travel. He put down his paper
And called me a coward.

You just run away from life.
If you were brave
You'd stay home.
My father wasn't brave,

He did not like to travel or me.
But for my job, for my pleasure,
My whole career, I crossed continents
Let mountain ranges rise and fall

Beneath the airplane windows,
Like waves in the ocean.
Now my passport aches
To be stunned with strange stamps

Gone are the frenetic
Nights of watched clocks
And snatched sleep along
With all the family events I missed,

For years, so I could cover
More distance, do more work,
Beat another deadline,
Interview one more stranger.

Now I am still,
Only trains travel past my window
And my heart beats in the darkness
Mossed with menopause and prayer.

I confront my static life
Harboring a family, being brave,
Facing down my father's voice,
Beg each word I meet,

To reboot old memories –
So I can commune with life,
Put down words that build, ignite,
Gallop over capitol landscapes.

I am brave. I do not travel.
Instead I ask each character I invent:
How did you get here?

SPARROW
after "Stork" by Ellen Bryant Voigt

Cathy Barber

They are so ubiquitous people call them
LBJs: little brown jobs. Most cozy
to civilization. House Sparrows
build nests in walls and roofs.
Chipping Sparrows sculpt nests
with hair. There are Vesper Sparrows,
White-throated Sparrows and
Grasshopper Sparrows. The Hedge Sparrow
is not a sparrow but the White-rumped
Snow Finch is.

In Indonesia, if a woman spies a sparrow
on Valentine's Day, she will find happiness
marrying a poor man. In ancient Greece,
they, birds of love, drew Aphrodite's chariot.
Christians believe the sparrow loyally
stayed with Christ through crucifixion.
Ancient Egyptians believed they
caught the souls of the dead
and carried them to heaven.

Mao went about eliminating the seed eaters
in the Great Leap Forward's
Kill a Sparrow Campaign.
Peasants smashed eggs, shredded nests,
shot them from the sky,
banged pots and pans
to exhaust the sparrows,
too frightened to land.

Locusts devoured the crops.

SPEAKING TO BEES

Joan Colby

Bees dislike consternation.
They go peacefully about their tasks.
Each knows its obligation
To the hive. Feeding the queen who loves them
If love is the gift of life.

Bees resent disturbance,
Sudden traffic or an unspoken
Quarrel that troubles the air
In which bees pursue sweetness.

Take care to be calm
For the sake of bees who dislike anger,
But are easily angered, an irony
That would mystify bees in their
Pursuit of simplicity.

Go veiled among bees like women
Who donate their sons to history. Like nuns
Who honor silence. Once the bees
Offer their trust, you can walk
Naked in their realm unstung
Like this woman who talks to bees
In a quiet confiding tone.
She tells them everything,
Not just who has died.

The bees uphold the world
With perpetual industry.
The collapse of hives is like
A vast caldera erupting
In a cloud that might cancel sunlight
For generations.

Remember the man in the woods
Clothed in bees.
When he screamed his mouth
Choked with the buzzing.
The hoofbeats of his vanishing horse
Echoed the intrusion
Cantering under the trees
As the bees swarmed
With their new militant queen.

Each hive houses three thousand bees,
A fervent alchemy,
Corporation of golden souls
Entombing their plunder in wax.
A museum of everything we hold
Precious—the pollinated world
In which millions of people are kissing.

THIS ALMOST NIGHT
(After *Man and Woman Contemplating the Moon*
    by Caspar David Friedrich)

Adele Kenny

It's the way trees darken before the sky ... this almost night ...
another side of time and new. We think in pauses and, in those
pauses, everything (it seems) is suspended or standing still. The
moon, rising, reorders the sky, drifts and slips through clouds—
sliver of moon, its nimbus pale, like a word almost spoken.

A night bird shapes its wings to the wind and lifts its shadow away
from the world, a world gone white with the ghosts of our passing.
And this: the thought almost remembered (what we might have
kept)—a sky dimmed to November gray, and us moonstruck—
what we thought we knew, the emptiness we didn't see coming,
this sack of rocks slung over memory's shoulder.

THE DARKEST DAY

Joyce Meyers

As the light shrinks, people
shop for trinkets, bits
of brightness to ward off
the night. No one thinks

of black holes, dark matter
hovering, but everyone
notices how early the moon
hangs low, telling

nothing of what it knows.
Strings of electric colors
hang, candles burn,
a frantic yearning

for assurance that light
will return. Solstice,
the sun standing still,
the moment before

it seems to shift, bring
gradually lengthening days
toward spring, the birth
of everything bursting

from the womb of earth.
Has there ever
been doubt? Never
in the memory of man

has the sun failed
to come carrying
its basket of brilliance.
Easy to forget how history

is merely a blink
in the eye of time,
that the sun, like us,
was born to die.

ASHES IN THE RIVER

John Grey

My one regret
is that we didn't toss his ashes
in this river,
the slow meandering stream
that was his habitat
more than the cottage,
certainly more than any funeral home
and hole in the ground.

What more could we have asked for
than a sky as clear as this,
sun lightly breaking apart the surface
to reveal the fish, the diadems within.

An urn, a prayer, a blessing
and his favorite fishing ground –
he could drift as lazily as the line he cast,
the peaceful moments he created
just by being in this place.

But others preferred ritual
to rose petals and daisies
tossed into the current
for accompaniment.
But how could a long line of dark cars,
a priest's solemn intonations,
match the speck of dust
on a momentary swell,
the color filling out his journey.

Someone said
a stone is permanent,
ashes in the steam
end up as trout food.
He had no idea
how judiciously
he made my case.

GIVING THANKS

Linda Fischer

Up at dawn the day after Thanksgiving
just as the sky's ragged hem begins to ignite.
I've managed it again—strained the capacity
of my inadequate dining room by shoehorning
a second table in on one end, mounted
the customary turkey (graced by all the trimmings),
baked the pumpkin pie, added a second apple
(for insurance) and fatted my extended family
into the usual stupor by nightfall—a duty
I expect will devolve upon me for as long
as I can heft a 20-lb. bird into the oven.

Felicitous indeed is this rite of culinary plenty:
chicken liver pâté (*de rigueur*), my mother's inviolable
stuffing, her potatoes crisped to a turn, and the tooth-
jarring cranberry conserve my mother-in-law
has passed along—traditions I preserve—yet how
satisfying to duck out of the kitchen for a window
of repose. Only the leftovers to consider now,
I suppose—oddments of turkey tucked into pot pie,
the carcass relegated to a fragrant soup brimming
with carrots and noodles—and my one piece
of domestic wisdom: cook and they will come…

IT IS GETTING HARD TO BREATHE, AMERICA
—*Jared Smith*

George Drew

I was born in the middle of the second
  great war almost in the middle
   of the greatest scientific century,

and because I sit here a few years
  into another of consequence looking
   back at the suddenly shrunken one

I was born into, how strange it is
  to be re-viewing it: Like an ocean
   it recedes ever farther, falling

backwards into the gray swells of time.

How strange to talk about the middle
  of a century here just past
   the perimeter of two of them—

that century my cradle, this one my crypt.

ADVICE FROM THE SPOON

Luray Gross

The best mirrors distort; don't try to be clever.
Respect the knife and the fork, but grovel in front of neither.

A mouth is a cave you will enter and enter;
you are only a worker, never a guest.

Depend on the testimony of others: sugar is sweet,
but you will not taste it. Nor will you taste the bitter remedy.

Silver tarnishes, pewter bends, iron rusts:
look to wood for grain shaped by time.

Nest with your fellows. Despise not
those larger or smaller than yourself.

You will make no music on your own.
Curve and turn, scoop and carry.

Your edge scraped against the famine bowl
plays a song sweeter than any other.

Be kind to smooth gums, be they old or young.
Offend not the mouth guarded by many teeth.

For resting, the floor is suitable as the table or drawer.
Allow the one who holds you to find your balance point.

If you think you were born to be filled,
remember you were born to be emptied.

FALCON

by Elise A. Miller

The lake needed to be dredged; it wasn't just a ploy to get the association to spend more money, the way George complained it was between shouts of praise at his son Falcon, for doing a thing any kid his age could do.

"Fantastic job, Son!" he called to the boy, one of those underweight children with translucent skin that let the veins show through. Under-ripe.

Falcon was taking his turn on the zip-line, really an old iron hook on a pulley, something you could buy in an antique barn along Route 611. The hook pulled the rope so low in the middle that Falcon was forced to raise his feet to his head, knees splayed, hair dragging the ground so the leaves could weave their way in. Falcon, who called his dad 'Father,' and said things like, "Definitely not," and, "I am six and seven-quarters." A miniature dandy, a capsized contortionist scrolling through the air between two black walnut trees.

"Father, did you see me?" he shouted from the ladder leaning against the tree when he landed, a crown of dried leaves encircling his head.

"I sure did son. That was amazing." George turned to me then and I saw that flicker in his eye, even though I was almost certain he was gay. The flicker that said, do you find me attractive? "There is nothing wrong with the retaining wall," he said to me. "They are not getting another penny from me for that." I took a step back but nodded. Bluster frightened me.

After lunch we walked to the lake—George, Falcon and me. Peaches and Spike stayed back at the cottage with Mark. They were still zip-lining, addicted. I decided I needed a break, and was planning on a nice relaxing walk to the waterfall. I'd walk with George and Falcon for something to do. Plus, I was determined to suss out whether or not George was gay once and for all. It was eating at me. Because he aroused me and I wanted a fantasy fuck, but it had to be believable. It was just the way my mind went.

The workers already started on the lake. There was a crowd gathered on the dock, the one where the diving board used to be, the one that shadowed the colony of tadpoles. A crowd at a dredged lake. It wasn't typical. Lake dredging wasn't news. It was nuisance.

The three of us began to approach but one of the older ladies waved us away. "Keep the boy back," she hissed, then placed one hand over her mouth, the other on a gold crucifix that hung over her souvenir T-shirt.

I looked at George, who gripped Falcon's hand. "What is it father? Have they found a whale?"

"I'm not sure son, but I just remembered. We have to get back to the cottage. Let's go. Say goodbye." George nodded at me and walked off with his son and I was none the wiser. I'd have to conjure those Vampire Diaries boys again.

Falcon waved at me, craning his neck to see the whale he suspected washed up to shore in this tidy man-made lake in the Poconos.

I approached the dock. Now I could see that the women, and even a few of the men were crying, wiping their sagging faces with liverspotted hands. Then I saw why. Tangled in the swampy grass, a rock tied to her waist with a length of clothesline, was a woman, or what was left of one. Something had nibbled her toes and fingertips. Her lips were gone too. Eyes, eyelids. Her clothing was intact, except for her right breast, which lay there dead and defiant, sticking out from her pistol-emblazoned tank-top. It was a perfect, beautiful breast, my favorite sort, with a small nipple, and full on the underside. I guessed she'd worn a C-sup if she ever used a bra at all. She wore jean shorts too, the kinds that some girls seemed to love—waist high and so short your ass cheeks hung out below. Her hair was still blond, the remains of her face bloated and kind of dented looking. One of the workers held a single platform sandal in his hand, offering it to the sky, a meager question mark. "I never…" he said, and then again: "I never…." He held the shoe and walked to the shore. Then he dropped to his knees and vomited, still clutching the shoe.

That's when Falcon returned, having wriggled from his father's grasp. The boy wormed his way to the front of the crowd the way short people do. He peered over the edge right in front of me, hands pressed to his unscathed knees. I had the urge to place my hands over his eyes. Guess who? I'd say.

"Father!" he cried. "Come quickly! Miss Cashmere Blue is down here and she needs your help!"

George swooped in, gripped Falcon's shoulders. I was pushed out of the way, which I resented, even with the whole corpse discovery. And I could feel the trembling of this man who had never been in a situation like this before. "Son," George said, pretending himself authoritative. "You know this woman?" His voice cracked. Emotion overtook him. Gay, I thought, defiant.

"I certainly do, Father. She read my palm. She told me my future."

The group of weepy adults turned toward Falcon, leaning in, tears dropping onto the top of his head.

"Where did you meet her?" George asked, kneeling, squeezing Falcon's tender arms.

"I see her booby," Falcon said gravely.

"Where did you meet her?" George repeated, desperation hijacking his voice.

"Right over there." Falcon looked to the woods, where the canoes were kept. "Remember? We were digging to China and I needed a pine cone to send down the chute, and I ran into the woods right there to retrieve one."

"How come you didn't tell me?"

Falcon shrugged his narrow shoulders. "She promised me I couldn't. Or my future wouldn't come true. Come to pass, is how she put it. Is my future doomed now, Father?"

"Absolutely not, son. Is there anything else you can tell me about her?"

Falcon scanned the faces around him. Then he looked at the dock between his sandals. "I cannot say. I might upset some people here. Oh father, can someone make her booby go away?"

Falcon sobbed then, and pressed his face into his father's shorts, into his baggy crotch.

George stroked Falcon's hair. His eyes shone with impotence.

"Oh Father," Falcon sobbed. "Miss Cashmere is gray and her mouth and eyes are disappeared, and her booby is popped out and scaring me." He turned his face up toward George. "Do you think it was the puppets?"

"The what?" I asked, unable to silence myself, unable to predict whether Miss Cashmere's dead body or her exposed breast would cause Falcon the most trauma as he grew older.

"The puppets," Falcon explained, turning to me and considering the depth of my ignorance. "I'm speaking of the puppets who live in the sun. That's where they come from. They drop out on strings." Duh, his tone said.

George turned to me and said, "I can't figure out where he knows it from. He says it was school but I had a conference with his regular teacher and his bible teacher and neither one has heard of it."

"It's okay," I said, placing a hand on his shoulder. George bundled me up in his arms then, cried into my shoulder unabashed, all while Falcon sobbed into the man's crotch. It was awkward. Gay or not, I might never know. I hugged him hard.

The murdered, half-exposed fortune teller below us continued to decay as we stood embracing above her. "The strings would burn," I said into George's shoulder, feeling tears rise.

"No they wouldn't," Falcon said below me. "It's magical, something you wouldn't understand. You're too old."

I stepped back and shot the boy a look, felt compelled to flash him both of my breasts.

"Now son, be nice. Apologize to Mrs. Morgan." George looked into my eyes. I wanted to kiss him.

"I apologize," Falcon said, but he didn't mean it. The kid thought me an idiot. I thought him deranged. Nothing wrong with that, but he was rubbing me the wrong way. I thought I might just kick him over the edge of the dock, but then he said, "Your daughter is a goddess, Mrs. Morgan. I'd like to marry her. May I?"

I opened my mouth but no sound came out. A woman was dead and I was considering a marriage proposal from a six-year-old. Well, six and seven quarters. "Thank you," I said. "Let me think about it." I tried to smile at George over this admission of love, but he was staring at the body. Gay or not gay? I hated that I had to know.

"I'm in love with Miss Lovey Dove," Falcon said, swooning between us. "Miss Lovey Dove can rescue me and deliver my future!" Then he turned back to the corpse. "Oh I can barely look," he said, staring.

"Jesus is with her now, Son."

I stopped myself from shaking my head in anger. Lest ye be judged, I scolded myself, and thought about how confusing it must be to be gay and Christian. I knew people did it all the time but it still baffled me. It seemed so masochistic.

"Oh, Jesus!" Falcon said, with longing in his reedy little voice.

"What did she say, Falcon, about your future, what did she tell—" I began, when a hissing sound from below caused us all to recoil. The corpse had off-gassed and a stench bubbled from her depths that nearly toppled me. I breathed through my mouth and watched her deflate through the blur of my watery eyes. I could not turn away. Nothing this astonishing ever happened in Lake Heaven. I squeezed my cell phone, itching to snap a picture and text it to Mark. But it didn't seem like the right time.

Our small memorial crowd remained there as the workers milled around us, cleaning up for the day, as the ambulance and the police and even a chartreuse fire truck arrived. One by one we were questioned and then released as the sun dipped low over the pine trees on the lake's far edge.

Then it was just George, Falcon and myself, standing on the dock, staring at the spot where the corpse had lain before she was collected by the professionals. The boy looked into the clouded sky as a great blue heron landed in the swampy remains of the lake and surveyed us, its black stick feet sinking into the freshly revealed mud.

"See?" Falcon said. Pointing at the bird. "The strings do not break."

"Are they invisible?" I asked, bending at the waist, so that the boy might glimpse my cleavage.

"Obviously, Mrs. Pea Brain," he said, peering between my breasts, and George requested a second apology.

FIXING THINGS

by Roger A. Lopata

We had agreed I would take a cab from the airport, but there is no mistaking the maestro in his black cape, all six feet seven inches of him, fedora-topped, looming above the crowd as he studies the flight information monitors.

I slip alongside him. "What are we looking for?"

"Your flight from Cuttyhunk," he says without turning to address me. He waves at the flickering screens with a flourish that ends in a glissando of his long fingers. "There are no flights from anyplace called Cuttyhunk. So, how am I supposed to meet your flight from Cuttyhunk?"

"Providence. I told you I was flying from Providence and that I'd take a cab."

"You said Cuttyhunk,," he says with exasperation. "As if I could make up a name like that? And you can't afford a cab."

Neither of us has taken his eyes off the screens to look at the other. "I wouldn't have said Cuttyhunk. It doesn't have an airport, and you know I can afford a cab."

My father turns, looks down at my five feet, eleven inches, and winces. "You got a suit?" I hoist my duffel bag to indicate I'm neither as slovenly nor doltish as he suspects, but he shakes his head. "It'll be all wrinkled in that thing. Don't you have a proper suitcase?"

"It's Permanent Press," I say, not telling him I bought the suit five years ago on the occasion of his seventieth birthday thinking then it would only be a matter of time before I would be coming home for a funeral.

"Permanent Press," he mutters. Shaking his head, my father turns toward the parking garage. "If Jules hadn't died, that would've killed him."

"It's good to see you, too, Pop," I say, following the fluttering edges of the cloak he wears despite the sunny warmth of late spring. A slight shuffle has infiltrated his gait. He still has the same imperious bearing with which he would strut out onto the concert platform, but his pace is slower, and to me his speed always contributed to his enormity. He would not simply set himself before a Steinway Concert Grand; he would envelop it, subsume its eight feet, eleven and one-half inches with an authority that conferred possession not just of the piano, but the entire orchestra. For my father, shuffling is not just incongruous; it is impossible.

Uncle Jules's death had not been unexpected. Several months ago, my mother had telephoned with news of the stroke that had left him paralyzed on one side and severely aphasic. "Nonsense," my father, who was on an extension, interrupted her. "They need to get him up out of that bed and moving around. Physical therapy…"

"He can't move, honey," my mother suggested.

"Nonsense," my father recapitulated. "He can move if they make him. They're babying him." And, as usual, the call devolved to their duet with me as audience, listening to comments fly back and forth like dueling virtuosi. But I made a mental note to make sure I still had the suit.

Leaving the garage, my father pays and starts rolling up his window. The glass ascends jerkily at a forty-five degree angle. "What's wrong with that window?" I ask.

"Nothing." With a graceful right overhand, he seizes the window and gives it a sharp tug. It dutifully straightens out and rolls up the rest of the way. "We should go straight to Jules's," he announces, taking a quick, disdainful look at me as if to confirm his recollection, "but Sarah can't see you like that. We'll go home and you'll change…" He waits through a pause of several beats. "…into your permanent press suit."

It would be pointless to explain that I could not risk wearing the suit on the ferry that operates between Cutty-hunk and New Bedford, pointless to show him my pants, stained from the salt spray we picked up crossing Buzzards

Bay. Never having deigned to visit me in the twelve years I have lived there operating what I like to think is a successful, well-known, boatyard, my father would not understand this. To him, my work, indeed, anything outside the narrow corridor between Philadelphia and New York, exists only in some ethereal sense, places he need not see, and that, to him, do not exist.

"They killed him at that damn hospital," he mutters as we careen through the warren of South Philadelphia back streets he uses as shortcuts, eschewing the Schuylkill Expressway and I-95. To him, the city's original grid of streets laid out by William Penn three hundred years ago remain a sacred text, the highways, modern abominations he will not acknowledge. When Uncle Jules moved to a penthouse in Center City, my father would neither speak to him nor visit for weeks, not because of the ostentation of the place, but because it was in one of the first buildings to violate the century-old gentlemen's agreement that no structures in the city would ever be built higher than Penn's statue atop City Hall. Such is my father's compact with the past. I do not believe he has ever played the work of a composer born after 1930.

He continues snaking wildly through the narrow streets. As we speed through the intersection of Passyunk and Federal for the third time I begin to suspect he is lost. "Don't you need to take a left over to Grays Ferry?" I ask.

"I know where I'm going," he snarls, throwing us violently into the left turn he has missed twice already. The maestro has never been one to take direction well.

As we pull into the driveway of the West Philadelphia Victorian where I grew up, a home my parents had spent years painstakingly restoring, I notice paint peeling from some of the gingerbread. A section of gutter hangs from the eaves. I am wise enough to say nothing.

It was only natural that, at age 14, I rebelled against all things musical. I remember my father's odd mixture of bewilderment and fury when he discovered I had become truant from my thrice-weekly lessons at the Curtis Institute of Music. Realizing no monthly bill had arrived, he phoned and learned I had stopped attending the four-hour sessions of practice, theory, and history I had grown to loathe.

"I hate it," I told him. "What good will it do me to memorize sonata-allegro form or the names of all of Bach's children and grandchildren?"

The question baffled him. He stared at me, clearly unable to conceive how anyone could not want to study composition and practice for endless hours. "You must grasp the art in its totality," he said.

To which, of course, I answered, "What makes you think anyone in the world besides you would want to do that?"

I never had another piano lesson, never attended another of his concerts, not even when he was guest soloist for Leonard Bernstein's 45th Anniversary Gala with the Philharmonic. And I did not perform another remotely musical act until my junior year in high school when, completely indifferent to all things academic, I accepted my advisor's suggestion to take wood shop and was assigned a dulcimer as a semester project.

I had never worked with tools – the only kind of hammer available or discussed at home struck a piano string – and, since abandoning music, I had done little with my hands. Yet I found an immediate satisfaction in the tactility of wood, in the silent beauty of the grain, and was stunned by the pleasure I discovered in transferring the delicate curves from the plans to a form and then carefully bending thin steamed strips of cherry around it. I still remember my delight in watching each coat of shellac bring out its rich, deep color.

Yet the dulcimer's open tuning made the instrument boring. It was too simple, and my antipathy for music was stronger than any desire to play my creation. My real pleasure lay in the thing itself, in looking at its graceful shape, the way reflections skittered across the planes of its surface, and the totally unanticipated joy I found in knowing I had made it.

I took pride, too, in one of the few "A's" I would ever receive. With studied carelessness, I left the dulcimer alongside my report card on the table in the front hall where we always put the day's mail. My father, without even picking up the instrument, looked at the report card and offered a dismissive wave, muttering, "Wood shop, for God's sake."

Neither did he notice that summer – being away at a series of guest appearances at Tanglewood and Wolf Trap – that, rather than joining my friends' families in their annual migrations to the Jersey Shore, I stayed home and worked six days a week with uncharacteristic dedication at the Philadelphia Maritime Museum performing any odious chore that was asked of me just to be near the plank by plank construction of a 30-foot Herreshoff ketch, whose building I had discovered quite by accident but that ultimately led me to my passion for wooden sailing craft.

Shortly after I had completed the dulcimer, one aimless teenaged Saturday I strayed from the gaudy attractions of South Street and wandered down to the Delaware River where I heard the unmistakable echo of a smoothing plane lapping back and forth. Still intoxicated with my newfound pleasure in wood, I was drawn toward the sound, following it onto the old pier that housed the museum's workshop. Shuffling inside I instantly lost hold of my carefully mustered teenaged ennui, transfixed by the boat, her nearly completed oak frames being crafted by a pair of serious-looking men. For hours, I stood, mesmerized, studying the plans that hung on the shop wall and turning to match them against the complicated shape on the shop floor, a bold sheerline with an exquisitely rounded canoe stern, named Rozinante by her creator, L. Francis Herreshoff, perhaps the most visionary yacht designer of the early twentieth century. Gradually, I began to see her, this 7,000-pound vessel that would someday dance across the water driven only by the wind, and just as gradually I recognized these men were transforming an inert set of lines into something real and, like my dulcimer, startlingly beautiful. And the boat had nothing to do with music. For the first time, my father began to recede from my life. Over the next several years, I would spend every spare moment at the shop, devouring all I could learn about ship's carpentry, attaching myself to craftsmen to study woodcraft, lofting, rigging, even sailmaking. After two lackluster years in community college, my grades trailing steadily downward as I spent all my spare time at the workshop, I told my bewildered parents I had decided to apprentice to a ship-wright in Massachusetts.

There, my teachers and I soon discovered my aptitude for interpreting and executing even the most arduous designs. Not unlike musicians who can sight-read difficult scores, I was able to read plans and not just see them three-dimensionally but also quickly divine their development into competent, well-organized projects. And I loved the work. From selecting timber, supervising its milling and drying, to each aspect of construction, whether hewing a mast or the hot, arduous task of steam bending ships' frames, I never tired of the labors. Several years later, when the owner of the yard decided to retire, everyone agreed it was only natural he offered to sell it to me.

I eagerly accepted, a decision I have never regretted, though it did consign me to life on an island with only 400 year-round residents, a close-knit community whose fellow-ship I generally enjoy but whose size has left me unmarried and, I suppose, somewhat insular. My closest friends remain the shipwrights with whom I work and Jerry Montgomery, who partnered with me seven years ago in purchasing the yard. Jerry oversees administration and marketing leaving me to my work, yet he tirelessly orchestrates romantic introductions for me with every unattached woman visiting from the mainland in summer. Indeed, the men in the yard have made a running joke of my vacant love life, subscribing me to online dating services, romance book clubs, and once posting a carved teak plaque reading "Spinster Shack" in front of the dilapidated waterfront cottage I bought near the yard and still intend to restore to its original Arts and Crafts brilliance, a project that always loses priority to our jobs in the yard but that, given my parents' fierce pride over their longtime Victorian home, guiltily nags at me each night when I return to it.

"Your mother is already there," my father grumbles, laying his keys on the table in the front hall. "We'll go join her after you get changed," he says, idly flipping through the mail just long enough for me to hear the pause, "into your permanent press suit."

After two decades, my parents have turned my old bedroom over to excess memorabilia and clutter that have spilled out of my father's crowded third-floor studio. Old scores, dog-eared and annotated in the dark lines of his heavy hand, lie piled on the desk and windowsill. Brief comments like, "alla breve!!!" or "NO!!!non andante – Mournful" overflow in the margins where he has stamped his own indelible style on a piece. I want to unpack, but the dresser drawers are stuffed full of more old scores. So I yield and simply take out the suit, a clean shirt, and a tie, leaning my duffel, which bears the Keppner and Montgomery Boatyard logo, up against the foot of the bed.

Originally we had made a few of these duffels in our sail loft as launch party gifts for the owners of new boats, but the steady trickle of requests we kept receiving made us consider selling them. The demand grew so quickly, we opened a retail storefront in the boatyard and expanded to a whole line of bags, t-shirts, caps, and jackets, all snatched up by well-heeled tourists who visit the island in the summer. Jerry has even begun talking about opening a café or coffee bar and calling it "The Boatyard," this on what, a decade ago, was a remote island but whose summer population has swelled grotesquely in recent years in an explosion of huge second homes and condominiums. Nowadays, a steady stream of visitors regularly hurries past the boats we have under construction stopping only to ask where the gift shop is. Though the men in the shop and I resent the intrusions, their casually free spending has become almost as profitable as the boats we build, so I accede without protest to Jerry's plans to cultivate the tourist trade.

Standing before the bathroom mirror adjusting my tie, I notice soap film has built up in the sink. Nothing here is quite as fastidiously tended as usual. Dust has accumulated on bookshelves; thin cobwebs inhabit corners of the ceiling. I worry that age has made my parents less attentive, then quickly transpose my fear into the hope that they will not notice this is the same tie I wore during my last visit.

When I emerge, my father merely looks at his watch and says, "We'd better get going." In truth he is only slightly more ill-tempered than usual, and I realize this may be his way of expressing grief. Though their relationship was marked by a ferociously combative sibling rivalry, my father and Uncle Jules shared a quiet, grudging respect for each other's accomplishments. Jules created a packaging company that made him imposingly prosperous, status he took pride in flaunting. Arguably, my father enjoyed even greater success in the arts, but this never brought affluence and therefore, to Uncle Jules, always remained of lesser consequence. At least, that is what my father complained of, constantly. And though my father seemed to disdain his brother's ostentation, a subtle jealousy always crept beneath his contempt. When Uncle Jules arrived for a visit one Sunday behind the wheel of a cream-colored Mercedes with hand-stitched kid-leather seats that caressed occupants so sweetly I wanted to ride in that car forever, my father huffed about conspicuous consumption, overpriced foreign products, and the company's murky connection to the Nazis. Yet for weeks thereafter, he scoured the classified section of The Philadelphia Inquirer until he found a used 300-SE which he purchased and lovingly maintained for years.

I know, too, from my mother's phone calls that my father, more than anyone else, had fought his older brother's death, even after a second stroke left him vegetative. As they let my uncle die per the terms of his living will, my father railed against the doctors and angrily accused my aunt of treachery. More than once, confrontations at the hospital between him and my cousin Richard, who, even in childhood seemed to be the inheritor of the abrasive Keppner temperament, became so loud that nurses had asked them to leave.

"They laid him down and killed him," my father hisses as we ride up the forty-two floors to Uncle Jules's penthouse. "You watch that smug bastard Richie. You'll see," he says with angry disgust. He stops in the hall and gives me a long look. "We'll go in the back door," he sighs, not bothering to knock and leading me into Uncle Jules's study. There, plaques honoring my uncle's expansive patronage and philanthropy cover the walls. Elaborately framed photos chronicle various groundbreakings, ribbon-cuttings, and galas in which he had somehow been instrumental. Directly behind the high-backed leather desk chair hangs an enormous photomontage chronicling his wife and children from the earliest days of their marriage to the birth of grandchildren. One small frame sits on his massive rosewood writing desk. Assuming it will be a portrait of my aunt, I am surprised to see a grainy old black and white snapshot of my father and Jules, posing on the stoop of the rowhouse where they grew up in South Philadelphia. Hair tousled but in their good clothes, my father still in knickers and the older Jules in a dark wooly suit, each one's arm stretches across the other's shoulder. Uncle Jules's face tilts up, catching the light. His head is thrown exultantly back, lips stretched into a broad, joyous smile. My father is looking up at his older brother, eyes wide and somber, but the beginnings of a smile rising on his lips, perhaps yielding to the contagion of Jules's high spirits. Seeing both of them so young, so open, their faces uncreased by worry or age catches me off guard. I had never known such exuberance and spirit in either of them and am struck by the photo's solitary presence on my uncle's desk. I do not know if my father has seen it. He is examining a matching Mont Blanc pen and pencil thrust like twin Excaliburs into a piece of Steuben glass etched with several musical bars in a gently curved scroll, beneath which reads the legend, "Jules Keppner – Millennium Circle Benefactor – Philadelphia Orchestra."

"Here," he says, handing them to me.

After a dumbfounded instant, I muster my voice. "I can't take these."

"Why not? Richie doesn't need them, and I'm sure you don't have anything like that," he says, opening one of the desk drawers and beginning to forage through its files. "Jules's will ought to be in here somewhere."

"You can't do that," I say, alarmed.

"Of course I can," he mutters without looking up. "This will be my job. I'll probably be meeting with the lawyer on Monday. There's going to be a lot of work to do. We'll have to start thinking about moving Sarah out of here and selling this place. She doesn't need all this space. We'll probably never get what Jules put into it. I told him when he bought it..." He continues thumbing through the manila folders, issuing a frustrated sigh.

"Don't you think the estate will be Richie's responsibility?" I wince as soon as I've said it.

"Richie?" he practically bellows. "That little schmuck?"

Terrified that someone will hear his tirade, I try to distract him. "Shouldn't we at least go pay our respects to Aunt Sarah?"

My father looks up at me and grunts. "Might as well. I can't find anything in here anyway."

As he steps into the hallway, I carefully put the pens back on the desk. By the time I catch up to the maestro, my cousin Richard is approaching. "Uncle Samuel, why are you using the back door?"

My father drops his cape and fedora into Richard's arms with a curt, "Hello, Richie." Tension tightens the corners of my cousin's mouth, and I jump between the two of them.

"Richard. I'm sorry about your dad," I say, self-conscious that it's all I can come up with. Though the same age, we are not close, estranged by our fathers' habit of measuring themselves against each other, even in their children's accomplishments where I, of course, sorely disappointed my father. How Uncle Jules must have gloated matching me, a mediocre student, who abandoned college to build boats that are seldom seen outside of a few harbors in New England to his own son, an athletic scholar who played football at Penn, went on to law school, and a career of impressive litigations that often lands his name and picture in the papers. And though wooden boats from Keppner and Montgomery are prized by aficionados, our sales are probably a fraction of Richie's annual billings. Still, I don't believe he and I dislike one another; rather our fathers' endless competition made any friendship between us untenable.

"Thanks," he says. "This has all been hard on Mom," he adds, glaring at the maestro.

But my father hasn't heard. He is racing down the hall crying out, "No," sidestepping guests, and galloping to the far end of the living room where some of the trays of food that dot the apartment have been set on the closed lid of the piano. At first I think he may simply sweep them onto the floor. But scooping them up, he drops them unceremoniously into the laps of a few guests seated on a nearby sofa, then whips a silk handkerchief from his pocket and begins delicately wiping the lid loudly muttering, "I can't believe this." He turns to a dumbstruck guest with a platter of corned beef and Swiss cheese on his lap. "This is a Bösendorfer 290," he lectures. "You don't put food on a Bösendorfer." Seeing the man's obvious bewilderment, he adds, "Would you doodle on a Cézanne?" His voice has grown louder. "You shouldn't even have the lid closed. The soundboard needs to breathe. It's Val di Fiemme." And, for a moment, I think he is going to fling the huge piano open, but my mother comes scurrying across the living room amid the small but growing buzz of voices.

"Sam," she says sharply. Others must always deferentially call him Samuel, maestro, or Mr. Keppner – only my mother uses the diminutive. And usually it works to silence him. But today, he will not be mollified.

"But it's a Bösendorfer," he growls, "And these…these thugs are using it like a deli counter." He ignores her as she takes him by the arm. "They respect nothing." His towering height makes my father's outburst inescapable. The living room has fallen silent.

Beside me, my cousin exhales a long, trembling breath, then walks across the room. For a moment, they stand, silent, uncomfortably close. "Uncle Samuel, please just leave," he says, fighting to keep his voice controlled, "Just leave this house. Now"

My aunt, a somber group of friends clustered around her, is blinking back tears, her hand drawn to her mouth. My other cousins, Richard's sister and brothers, stand nearby, their faces cast down to the floor. Guests shift uncomfortably back and forth on their feet in the penetrating silence. And my father. The color flushes deep in his face as he stares with incredulity at my cousin who tenders the hat and cape he still holds to my father.

Stunned as the rest of the room, I do nothing until I recognize the resolve in each man's eyes. Neither is about to yield. I dash forward, take the cape and hat from Richard, and seize my father's arm. "We need to go," I say, pulling firmly. Then, a collaborative pushing comes from the other side. It is my mother, and we shuffle silently out the door like some pathetic Vaudeville team in our awkward locomotion all the way down the hall and into the elevator, riding without a word to the garage where, defying convention, I climb into the driver's seat. My father does not protest, sliding into the back where he quietly begins muttering, "That son of a bitch. That no good son of a bitch."

"Sam," my mother tries to reason with him, "The boy just lost his father."

"And I lost my brother," he shouts. "Who does he think he is? That's not his apartment, you know. That's not his Bösendorfer."

"It's not yours either," my mother snaps, drawing a look of astonished disbelief from the maestro.

I can see he is pained, but I don't know if it is from her harsh rebuke or her suggestion that the Bösendorfer is not his. He has always coveted the instrument.

Even I was awed the day Uncle Jules invited us over to see what he described as his new toy. The Bösendorfer was massive, nine feet six inches, a full foot longer than most concert grands, carrying an extra nine keys, 97 instead of the usual 88, providing extra sub-bass notes all the way down to bottom C. A collective gasp issued from the three of us as we entered the apartment, my mother's and mine, I suspect, from its sheer magnificence, but my father's probably more from shock and resentment. Uncle Jules, after all, did not play the piano or any other instrument.

"Twelve hundred and fifty-five pounds," were his first words. "Do you know what it costs to air freight 1255 pounds from Austria?" My father staggered over to the Bosendorfer, his mouth grotesquely open, hands twitching at his sides. Watching him, Uncle Jules had beamed. "They wanted to ship it, but I wasn't about to wait for it to crawl over here on some boat," he said. "I know a thing or two about how long that takes."

I could see the reflection of the Bosendorfer's carefully strung bronze harp and soundboard gleaming in its lacquered lid. What extraordinary woods had gone into its construction, spruce, beech, maple, alder, limewood, beautifully clear and perfectly grained, not a blemish or an imperfection anywhere, like a Thoroughbred horse, so magnificent that even if one knew nothing about racing, just the sight of it was breathtaking. But I did know. Bosendorfer was the instrument against which others couldn't even be measured. Its extended keyboard was the only one in the world that allowed the performance of certain pieces written by Bartók, Debussy, and Ravel. The sound of a Bosendorfer was reputed to be without peer. And I had an inkling of its cost, more than $200,000, more than the Philadelphia Orchestra could afford, which was why my father performed on a Steinway.

Uncle Jules had strutted over to the piano and, with his index finger, made a quick run, from low C all the way up the board. The sound was incredible.

"Well, Sammy," he had said. "What do you think? Isn't she a beaut?"

My father did not speak a word. And he never played Uncle Jules's Bosendorfer, never, never seated himself on its gleaming black bench, never even touched the keys, not that day nor ever. I don't know if anyone ever played it.

Driving home, I attempt to put down the window to get some fresh air in the car, but it sticks at the same crazy forty-five-degree angle as when we left the airport. "What's wrong with this window, anyway?" I ask.

"There's nothing wrong with it," my father shouts.

And from there, we ride in silence, the only sound the faint ticking of his keys in the ignition swinging back and forth against the steering column, quiet metronomic tapping, rekindling in me the pain of endless hours on a hard piano bench, enduring an ever-greater tedium as I angrily fought not to concentrate, mustered every available shred of clumsiness to make my playing sound even worse, an insolence that only served to decelerate time to an excruciating lento, every beat of the metronome hanging in the air. God, how I had grown to hate the piano.

Later I would find my own rhythm in the cadence of wood, the smooth slide of a plane lapping back and forth, the gentle push-pull of a saw, the resonant tap of a mallet, a state where I could lose myself for hours, day after day, for the months, sometimes years, it may take us to finish a boat in the yard. Often, after drifting in that gloriously focused state through an entire day, breaking for a late dinner though I am barely hungry, I want to believe that I have finally found a connection with my father, that this must be what he feels when he cloisters himself alone with his work. Yet I know, too, it is something he would be utterly uninterested in hearing me attempt to explain.

He wordlessly gets out of the car ahead of us, and by the time my mother and I are walking slowly up the driveway, he has hung his hat and cape on the hall tree and is disappearing up the stairs, retreating to the sanctuary of his studio.

My mother turns to me. "The funeral is tomorrow." The first words she has spoken to me since my arrival. Tending to the maestro has really been her life's work and not an easy task, trailing after him, mending the fissured relationships he generates with everyone from conductors and record company reps to his accountant, even the mail carrier. Almost as an afterthought, she adds, "Are you hungry? Do you want something?"

I can see how pale she is, how the skin sags around her eyes, and, not wanting to add to her burden, I shake my head. "I'll just go upstairs and get out of this suit. Why don't you take it easy for awhile?" She looks relieved.

In my old room, as I remove my jacket, I can hear the familiar sound of my father's piano bench shuffling back and forth on the floor above me as he settles at the keyboard. Opening the closet to look for a hanger, I find that it, like the rest of the room, is piled with boxes, files, old scores, and memorabilia. At eye level is a cardboard box, its original labeling, Deutsche Grammophon, scratched out, and the name "DAVID" written above it in heavy black ink. A shipping label reveals it once held copies of Chopin's Piano Sonata Number Two, a performance that won my father a Grammy nomination for Best Solo Classical Recording in 1980. The continued shuffling of the piano bench above assures me I will not be interrupted, so I peer inside.

On top is the at-once familiar cover of a two-year-old Inc. Magazine in which the Keppner & Montgomery Boatyard was listed as one of the top 500 small businesses in America. I'm stunned that my father has a copy. A yellow Post-It note marks the page featuring a photo of Jerry Montgomery and me standing alongside a just-completed Herreshoff sloop, our staff fanning out behind us on either side of the boat and a headline that reads, "Reviving the Art of Wooden Boats With Modern Management and Old Fashioned Care." On the Post-It, in the maestro's hand, is written, "Copy to J." The box is packed with more clippings, a copy of Wooden Boat magazine that detailed the launch of a 60-foot schooner we built for a free-spending telecom executive from New York, other articles, launch announcements, all the way down to small mentions of me or the yard from a hodgepodge of publications, each stickered with a similar yellow flag bearing the same notation, "Copy to J," and I dig down through all of them. My mother must have served as the press service, since my father would never bother himself with such tedium, and J, of course, was Jules. Every single one of these articles was for my uncle.

To the maestro, my work would always remain significant only insofar as it could serve him in his never-ending contest with his brother. Indeed, somewhere in Uncle Jules's condo, I imagine lies a similar trophy file for my cousin, both of us nothing more than reflections of our respective father's vanities.

I have burrowed deep into the box and am examining a yellowed clipping from the Philadelphia Inquirer about the Maritime Museum's summer intern program that featured a photo of the completed Rozinante under sail on the Delaware when I hear the floorboards creaking above me. Footfalls. The maestro is pacing. For all the time I have been exhuming this odd pantheon of my past, he has been sitting at his Steinway, silent. I cannot ever remember him not immediately plunging into some piece to match his mood, furious Rachmaninoff or strangely pensive Busoni. Nothing ever stilled his peripatetic assaults on the keyboard. But now he stalks back and forth above me in silence that, as soon as I am aware of, I find painfully unnerving. Something is not right.

Hastily replacing the box in the closet and draping my suit over a chair, I tumble downstairs still buttoning my shirt, striding through the empty kitchen, and out the back door to escape the quiet. In the yard my uneasiness only grows. It is not as though I have not stood here before, alongside this house and recognized it is no longer my home, but today, without the sound of his playing emanating from within its walls, looms the ominous prospect that it will not be his much longer either, and suddenly all I want to do is flee to my shop, sink into the familiar scent of wood, varnish, and paint, the warm feel of a plane or a chisel in my hand, tumble back into my own life. But I cannot, and I do not know what else to do.

Beneath the porch is a seldom-used stepladder that has lain there ever since we moved in, so old, it is made of oak, not the pine or hickory used nowadays. It has weathered to a fine patina and feels comfortable to my hands as I carry it around to the front of the house and set it beneath the dangling gutter. Climbing up, I find an accumulation of twigs, leaves, and muddy gunk. Who knows how long since the gutters were cleaned? All the extra weight has wrenched out several of the spikes and ferrules that hold the gutter to the eaves. I scoop out the debris and toss it into the overgrown bushes below, but it is clear that reattaching the gutter will require a hammer and none will be found in my parents' house, so I retrieve a good-sized rock from the garden. It has a nice flat face and is a good fit to my hand. I climb back up and lift the gutter into place carefully refitting each of the spikes. Steadying myself on the ladder, I draw back my arm and swing hard, giving the first spike a straight, clean blow. The metal gutter peals with a resonant gong. I strike again.

"Hey." My father's head protrudes from the third floor window, his face dark with irritation. "What the hell are you doing down there?"

Arm cocked in mid-swing, exasperated he can't guess, I mutter. "I'm fixing your gutter."

"There's nothing wrong with that gutter," he shouts. Before I can reply, his head withdraws back into the house.

It takes several more blows to drive the first spike. As I prepare to start on the second, the familiar first eight-bars of the Goldberg Variations drift down from my father's window.

Such a simple beginning, an effortless little dance tune embellished with a few baroque flourishes. But from that facile introduction evolves a cycle of thirty exhausting, maddeningly demanding exercises they say Bach penned for his pupil, the young virtuoso Johann Goldberg. My father knows them by heart. All my life, he has found in their perfect execution a kind of sanctuary, eyes closed, head lolling in delighted rhythm. When I was young, he would play the Goldbergs for me, swaying on the bench as he tirelessly ascended through them. His right and left hands mesmerized me as they flawlessly marshaled the two competing voices that characterize each variation, and at each one's end, after soaring through Bach's seamless eight-bar phrases that subtly slip from tonic to dominant to relative and back to the tonic key, he would open his eyes, look at me intently, and give an almost imperceptible nod, a gesture he never explained, but that in the painful beauty of Bach's peerless invention I always understood to mean that I would never even approach the talent demanded by the Goldbergs, and that I should never try.

Even now, hearing his liquid hands flow into the first variation, I can still see him executing that nod as clearly as if it were thirty years ago and I was sitting opposite him shame-facedly staring at my feet. God, how he could play.

Some say it would have been impossible for the young Johann Goldberg, at age 14, to have played the Variations, that no prodigy, regardless of his talents, could have played so mature a work. Others have suggested that the boy never existed at all, that he is, in fact, a fiction, that Bach wrote the Variations to be played by none but himself, that for all the 20 children he fathered, for the multitude of young students he taught, Bach respected no one quite so highly as himself. I find some sense in this when I think of my father. But I know what those historians have never suggested: what a lonely existence it must have been for Bach and what a sad mark it must have left on those around him.

I work my way across the roofline, climbing down to reposition the ladder, then clambering back up to drive more spikes. In the humid air, I break a sweat, staining the rock dark where I grip it, and I suddenly wonder, could his nod have meant something completely different? Could I have misread? In those dark eyes, in that subtle bow of his head, could there have been encouragement rather than disdain, a blessing, sanctifying me to blossom as a few historians contend Bach's young protégé Goldberg had? No. The maestro compelled me into service at the keyboard because it was what he thought a father was supposed to do, not because he saw any real talent in me (and, in truth, there was none), and certainly not because he wanted me to develop into any kind of real artist. Perhaps he could have tolerated a minor prodigy, maybe even taken some delight in it, but anything more would have been too great a threat to his own dominion. The Maestro Keppner plays, I tell myself, taking another swing with my stone, and I build boats.

And that is when I hear him falter. He is in Variation Number 20, the wildly gyrating, hand-crossing toccata, perilously dueling voices, perhaps the most challenging of the exercises Bach penned for his extraordinary young pupil. True, it is far into the Variations, after a series of trios that are both physically and emotionally draining, but in thirty years, I have never before heard him err playing it. It is only a small slip, a missed transition in the tonic, and he plays through it so quickly it would probably escape the notice of all but a few listeners. But I hear it, and I can hear his heart instantly leach from the playing. As he moves into the 21st Variation, there is nothing left.

Even though the 21st is in a minor key and marked Andante or "slow," most scores also add the notation con moto, acknowledging that it still must be rendered "with motion." Yet the sounds now seeping from the third-floor window are little more than a collision of tones, so mechanical, so forced that the G minor does not even sound mournful. It is simply empty, and I swing the rock hard to drown him out.

As the maestro knew them from memory, I had never seen the Goldberg's score. But once, shortly before I lapsed from my studies at the Curtis Institute, evermore infuriated at what seemed to me to be his boastful renderings of them, I retrieved a copy from the Institute's library, hoping to find some trick, some notation that revealed they were actually child's play, simple ten-finger exercises. Of course, there was none. Even as a novitiate, I could only marvel at the astonishing beauty of their intricacy, how in each of the thirty-two brief pieces Bach had begun with the same harmonic structure yet built each into a unique spiraling duet of left and right hands taking two voices ever deeper into an exploration of melody that always returned to the same beginning. In short, I was overwhelmed.

Balanced atop the ladder, I can still see the fearsome intricacy of the score and remember the awful sense of uselessness that swept over me the longer I studied it, a feeling that I never totally escaped until I was able to lose myself in the comparably magnificent plans of designers like Herreshoff whose boats, though a century old, still leave the most talented marine architects and engineers spellbound in their beauty and sophistication. In the building of those boats I finally found my own peace, a satisfaction, knowing that they were something he would never understand and that creating them was an act he could never perform.

And then there is silence. After the brief pause that should precede the 23rd variation, nothing. The maestro has stopped playing, has left the Goldbergs unfinished.

Slowly, I descend, waiting to hear him resume. Nothing. Working my way carefully through the bushes, I move the ladder over several feet and, in silence, begin climbing back up to fix what I can.

THE RED LADY

by Jodi Adamson

I'll kill her tonight. I've waited long enough. The other murder was weeks ago, and the police are still busy chasing their tails like one-legged hounds. I feel sorry for them sometimes. Stupidity reigns supreme. Yes, Halloween is a good night for killing my crimson sorceress.

I've watched her for weeks, carousing at McGriffins, a bar I frequent. Nobody saw my half-mast gaze peering over my beer at her arrival. The rest of the drunks mooed like a bunch of heifers begging to be milked. She was offering too.

Her slender form and delicate bones—encased in crimson red from her long mane to her spiked heels—stood out against the dusty walls of the bar. After entering, she perched on a swirling stool while her skirt inched up, revealing pale, freckled thighs. She turned to her first victim—a thick man, both of brains and brawn—who was ogling her red-tipped toenails. "Would you like to buy me a drink?"

She and her thick man drank and pawed each other as the light grew dimmer. Her schoolgirl giggle turned into a hyena laugh. His hands caressed some peeping cleavage. "No, no." She grabbed the offending finger and flung it away. "Drunk now. Must be going."

She jumped off the stool, landing precariously on her spikes. She turned her gray eyes and cocked her head as a red lock of hair fell on her nose. She pouted. "You can take me home." They left arm in arm.

I knew her pattern soon. She never varied. Always dressed as a tiny flame, leaving embers in her wake. Men who were sober or drunk. Clean-shaven or scruffy. Dressed in muddy overalls or sporting a Rolex. She led them out the door. Stupid girl. Doesn't she know that one of those fine gentlemen might slit her throat, leaving red rivulets all over her exposed flesh, as soon as she steps out of the safety of the bar's lights?

Which brings me back to now. My last victim's fear and shock is fading, leaving me in withdrawal, craving a fix only another murder can quiet. However, unlike the others, I yearn to follow my new lady out the door. See where she takes me before I take her.

Before driving to the bar, I count a wad of bills in my wallet and slide a switchblade into my pants pocket. I'm going to strangle her, but one must be prepared for any eventuality.

The sun throws out dying rays onto McGriffins as I arrive. A cardboard ghoul flies out of the shadows. I jump back. Snickers can be heard above the whiny jukebox music.

Rob, the bartender, laughs. "Thought you were a goner, Merv."

He pours my usual beer and slides it over. "What you doing here so early and not hiding in the shadows?" He points to my table in the back corner, now glowing orange due to a string of pumpkin lights hanging above it.

"I'm not fond of Halloween. Celebration of evil and things that go bump in the night."

Rob rolls his eyes and leans closer. "You want the red lady." He grins. "Good hunting."

I pass the hours sipping beer and wondering how the evening will progress. The murder is mine, of course, but I have left the rest up to her. Perhaps I will wrap my hands around her small neck after I have had my fill and twist. Let her cries of pleasure turn to pain. Let her beg for her life, although it will be hopeless. I shift on my stool while my glass slides out of my grasp. I need to remain calm. I distract myself by watching a drunken customer using a Dracula stand-up as a punching bag.

When my lady makes her entrance, she is dressed differently. Instead of flames, she has cloaked herself in midnight, invisible except for her hair. She stalks over to the barstools, hunting for prey, and finds me.

"Why the glare?"

She looks down at herself. "Vamp is a good look for me."

I recover quickly. "Yes, of course it is. Just used to seeing you in flames."

"I switched for Halloween. Skipped the fangs, though. A little too authentic—the blood." She smiles, showing pink teeth.

I smile. "Drink?"

I continue buying her red-colored drinks at her request. The shiny, red liquid wetting her lips gives me ideas I haven't had before. She prattles about poetry, philosophy, and the thin line between the dead and the living during Halloween. I block her words out and listen to her smoky voice, sometimes mentally inserting obscenities into her mouth.

"I feel my insides swimming. How lovely." She shuffles off the stool, pulling me along with her. She shakes her head with quick jerks and lets out a small burp. "Oops."

Tired of our drunken game, I ask, "Walk you home?"

A look passes quickly in her eyes, then disappears. "I'd be honored."

She doesn't make her move until we're away from the safety of the bar. The bright streetlights and the noisy trick-or-treaters are replaced by baying dogs and opaque bulbs on wobbly posts shining on cracked sidewalks. She turns toward me. "I know what you want. Gotta work for it, though. Follow me. Catch me." She giggles, eases her hands down her sides, and jerks her skirt up. A flash of skin and down again. She spirits away.

When I catch up to her, she is slumped over the barely visible white chalk outline of my last victim. I think she is vomiting but, as I approach, she looks up. "She died here. There should be blood."

I ignore the outline. Past crime scenes don't interest me. Instead, I grab my lady's arm. "There is no blood."

"You are so right. She was strangled. Like a chicken. Then she became a bloodless chalk outline. How sad."

"How sad." Memories of the chalk outline girl's murder rip through me, causing aches in several places. I tug on my girl again. "I followed and caught you. Now what?"

She scratches my face with her red-polished nails. "How do you think the earth felt on her body as they lowered her inside? Was it smooth and silky or rough and cutting?"

"She was in a coffin, dead. She didn't feel a thing."

"True but we can. Let's try it out."

"What?"

"The grave. See if I bleed. You want me? Commune with me and the spirits."

She is not only stupid, but kinky too. A grave? Wait, an open grave. On second thought, that will do nicely. A burial site already; perhaps her body never found. My blood pumps through my veins, and my legs jitter in anticipation.

"Kinky. I've never done it there before."

She claps her hands in delight as we head toward the cemetery.

By the time we enter the cemetery's rickety gates, my victim has left bits of clothing down the road like an X-rated bread crumb trail. Her unzipped dress is barely being held up by her breasts. Wiping sweat off my face, I follow her deeper into the cemetery.

I feel her eyes darting place to place as she tiptoes barefoot over the moist grass and loose soil. Suddenly, she confronts a yawning chasm reaching deep into the ground. I bump into her and almost send her flailing into the darkness.

"It's too deep. We'd never be able to get back up." She spins away toward the covered grave beside it. "Ah, let's do it here." Before I can agree, she's slipping off her dress and curling her body into the old, smelling earth like an innocent baby.

Divesting myself of clothing, I thrust down into her depths as she screams, her fingers white-gripped around the moldy headstone above her head. My hands snake around her neck and start to squeeze. I reach for my climax. She laughs.

"Really not into asphyxiation."

White-hot rage pours out of me, and I shake her like a rag doll. I notice her red hair pooling down around my arm. A wig! The long mane is replaced by a spiky, black mop.

Fireworks of memory explode in my brain. Another girl, my last victim, the girl under me all blur together. I go slack, which affords time for the pale legs clamped around my thighs to roll me into the open grave.

She's laughing, lying on her front, with her face perched in her hands. "You should see your face!"

After a few tries I manage to stand in the hole, glaring up at her. "Enough! Get me out of here!"

She smirks. "And what? Let you kill me? I don't think so. I'm afraid you're the one who's going to die." She rolls her eyes. "You are so clueless. Do I have to explain?

"This," she says, waving her finger around to encompass me and the hole, "is simple revenge.

"I've killed before. Men taken in by one thing. I admired your work until your work became my sister." She shakes her head, while I dig frantically for a grip in the dirt wall.

"I loved Megan. She never hurt a fly." She is locked inside some memory. "Chatting is over. Have to go. First, though, I have to finish holing you up. How gothic."

I hear her return with a shovel, and huge clots of dirt rain over my head. The dirt is soft and silky around my naked body.

I know it is hopeless because she is like me, but I plead one more time. "How will you explain my disappearance?"

I can't see her expression, but she is giggling again. "Why, a ghost got you, Merv!"

UNSEEN ANGELS

by Susanne Davis

That morning, I intended between morning and afternoon chores to walk the boundaries of the farm, to see what fences needed to be mended before we could put the cows to pasture. But the night before I had spent too much time and lost too much money at the casino and as I reached the southern most boundary of my old man's farm, I could not will my body back to chores but only forward, toward the horizon. I passed the old dump, the housing project, and the baseball field where I spent the hours of my childhood that weren't delegated to work. And, then I kept going further still. Past the old market, that had since become a Chinese market to accommodate the needs of the Chinese immigrants who worked at the casinos for next to nothing and lived like sardines in rickety houses along the city bus line. I kept going and going further still to the state road that ran to the casino, only I didn't go in that direction. I ran from it like a man being chased by demons. I crossed the highway and hitched a ride with the first trucker who stopped.

"Heading to New Jersey if you want to go that far," the trucker called across to where I stood on the road.

"Only to Windsor," I said, stepping closer. "Or as close as you go by there."

"No problem. Windsor, eh?" he asked.

I hopped up into the tall seat. I could hitch a ride there and back, and be back before afternoon chores. The cab was neat and tidy, smelled like apple tobacco and pine air freshener. The driver was a big fellow, over six feet. I could tell by the way his head grazed the roof above, with a build like a lumber jack. He stuck out his enormous hand.

"George." Medium brown hair was combed flat against his head and his face was square like the rest of him.

"Will," I said, taking his hand and giving it a quick shake.

"Did your car break down?" he asked.

I shook my head, but offered no further explanation of why I was hitching a ride to Windsor. But George glanced at me sideways. I could smell the manure on the cuffs of my jeans and the sweet smell of silage crusted around the hem as well. I could see he wanted to ask but being someone who spent long hours alone knew the importance of silence to a man who needed it. Still, when I saw how much he understood, it made me want to talk a little.

"You from these parts?" I asked.

George shook his head. "Louisiana, but I travel all over—East of the Mississippi mostly."

He raised an eyebrow. "So what's in Windsor?"

"I want to go check out a monument. It used to be here, in Uncasville. But then the Indians made a stink about it and it got moved to Windsor."

"Monument of what?" George asked. He reached forward and turned the radio off. It wasn't playing too loud, but loud enough to hear the faint melody of Johnny Cash sharing hard times and cold truths. I was glad he turned it off.

"Monument to whom," I answered. "John Mason."

"Who?"

"One of the first English settlers to this area." I don't know why it made me feel better that he didn't know the name. But it did.

"It was a bloody time, wasn't it?" he said. "But still, not too different from now. Things don't change much do they?"

"He was responsible for the slaughter of the Pequot Indians."

He flips down his visor. "Those were different times," he said. "The way we thought about the Indians."

"That's why they moved his statue to Windsor. The Indians didn't think it was right to have him there on their sacred burial ground."

He was glancing in his side mirror, switching lanes but he was listening and I appreciated that. It seemed to me that perhaps no one had listened to me for a long time.

Before I knew it he was leaning over to his glove compartment. He pulled out a bag of weed and some rolling papers.

"You smoke?" he asked.

"It's been a while," I said. It had been more than just a while. I was never much for drugs; I saw he kept a flask there as well, but he didn't offer it and before he flipped the compartment shut I spied the pistol lying beside the flask.

"You remember how to roll?" he asked, so that was how I found myself rolling a fat blunt and getting high early that cold April morning with George. I tried not to think about how much money I had lost the night before. I didn't let myself indulge too much because paranoia loomed at my shoulder and I wanted to keep my wits, what few I had left, about me.

We listened to George's music selection. He had a souped up stereo system, but the music was being streamed from his phone to his Bose Mini. Willie Nelson's voice filled the cab.

"Precious memories, unseen angels. Sent from somewhere to my soul...."

"Willie Nelson? And that was Johnny Cash earlier. You like the old timers."

"Willy Nelson's the man," George said. You know what he's done for farmers like you?"

"...sacred past unfold."

I wasn't a farmer though I came from a family of farmers. I wondered how George knew I was a farmer, but then I saw him staring at the cuff of my jeans. I had helped with chores just that morning because the farm hand hadn't shown up that day and my newspaper stories had been filed at the Bulletin the night before and I had the time free to help my old man milk, so I did. Now, I leaned my head against the window and closed my eyes, hoping George would just let the music be enough. I must have fallen asleep because the next thing I knew we were parked facing a green square and the statue of John Mason straight ahead.

I expected to feel something, some connection, but looking at the bronze statue of John Mason, his sword tilted down to the earth, I thought how lonely he looked, this guy who was doing the thing that he had been commanded to do, that seemed like the honorable thing at the time, slaughtering the Pequots and changing the course of American history, but history turned around so that the very sight of him was a scourge and an embarrassment.

I opened the truck door preparing to thank George, but to my surprise he opened his door too.

"Brought you this far," he said as though we had traveled half the country. "Might as well go with you to get a look at him. If you don't mind."

I said I didn't.

So we crossed the street and made our way over to the green. I pulled out my phone.

"So why do you want to see this guy?" George said.

I hesitated. "He's my ancestor."

"You want your picture taken with him?" George asked.

Who would want to make that kind of connection more memorable? "No, thanks."

"Go on. You got nothing to be ashamed of." He pushed me in front of the statue and I raised my hand over my brow to shield out the sun.

"You're not going to smile?" he asked.

"No."

So he took the photo and started fiddling with the cell phone to send the picture to his cell phone. We heard some noise and looked up to see a few kids circling George's truck. The passenger door was open and one of the kids leaned into the glove compartment.

"Get away from my truck, you little bastards!" George yelled. One of them was holding the Bose mini. "You drop it now or I'll shoot you fuckers!"

The kid with his head in the glove compartment popped up with the gun in his hand, waved it in the air, and released a shot.

Bang!

The teenagers laughed and scattered like cockroaches, leaving us with the echo of George's gun ringing out on Main Street.

"Get in," he shouted. We have to get that gun."

A siren rang out in the distance.

"What? Are you crazy?" I was shaking my head trying to understand, but I got in the truck. "Let's report them and let the cops get it back. It's them who should be running. They were stealing from you."

"The gun's not registered," George said, popping the truck into second gear. "Rather not get into it with the law." He reached under the seat and pulled up a semi-automatic.

"Holy Fuckin' shit," I said. "Is that one registered?"

He gave me a crooked grin. "You're pretty funny. Now roll down your window."

I did as he said and suddenly I wondered if his truck might just be full of guns.

"How's your aim?"

I hesitated and he shrugged. "No matter, you don't need to worry about accuracy with this." He tried handing me the semi. "We're going hunting."

The awareness of what he was saying spread slowly through my brain, like an oil spill. But I got it. Those teenagers were all dark skinned.

"This is no different than your ancestor," he said. "You got the legacy of your bloodline. And besides, they stole from me."

He gripped the wheel with one hand and the semi-automatic with another. When he had restarted the truck, Willie Nelson had restarted too and Unseen Angels was playing again now. George had to slow down just a bit to take the turn and I opened the door and leapt from the truck, dropping into a ball on my side as I hit the sidewalk. There was a storefront, I didn't even know to what, but I scooted into the entry. I needn't have worried because George didn't stop, didn't even slow down. He sped up. That's when I saw the confederate flag on his back bumper. Somehow I had missed it when I had jumped into his truck. I slipped into the store—it was an appliance store—just as the police cruiser came around the corner, lights flashing. They were on to George and I figured they'd get him before he got the teenagers, averting a tragic news story I wouldn't have to write.

I thought I'd steer clear of hitchhiking for a while, so I called a cab and as I sat in the back seat, we circled back around to the green, where John Mason's statue looked out and I thought then, maybe the natives had a point about removing symbols.

THE MAPLE ON PINE STREET

by Mike Cohen

It isn't nice to peek through other people's windows. You should resist the temptation, or settle for perhaps a furtive glimpse at twilight when interior lights have begun to come up and shades have not yet come down. There is one time of year when perfect strangers throw open their homes to the public. That is when the urge to discover what lies behind the walls of private residences can be satisfied openly, without risk of shame.

Connie and I seized the opportunity to take the open house and garden tour offered in May by the Society Hill Civic Association. We had seen several notable residences that offered appealing visions of past blending into present. Centuries old facades contain interiors that maintain a historical feel while incorporating the latest in style and functionality. Old exposed brick walls coexist with floating shelves. Wood-burning stoves share kitchens with stainless steel refrigerators. As our New Balance sneakers trod along old cobbled walkways, I was filled with a delectably haunting sense of lives and times gone by and Connie was filled with decorating ideas she had gleaned.

Together we were passing along Pine Street looking for the next house on the tour when from my peripheral vison emerged a sight that struck an ominous note. It was a large, gloomily looming figure on the other side of the street. I turned to look at what first appeared to me as a great black bird perched on the fence of an old cemetery. The fence was clearly leaning toward the sidewalk, so my immediate impression was that the gargantuan bird was weighing down the fence as if about to topple it over. A haunting admixture of images from Edgar Allen Poe's *The Raven* and *The Fall of the*

House of Usher conspired in my mind. Seized by momentary terror I was further appalled to find Connie was moving us toward the frightful creature. "No!" I exclaimed, instinctively pulling her back.

"What's the matter?" she said. "This looks like something interesting." Of course, Connie had not shared my frightfully fantastic impression. I blinked and looked again at the big "bird," which turned out not to be a bird at all. It was too big to be a bird, and as we went closer I could see it was not perched on the fence but stood just on the other side of the fence on the cemetery grounds. Amidst the shadows of the graveyard it became clear that the creature was some sort of statuary figure, tall and cloaked in black.

The cemetery was on the grounds of Old Pine Street Presbyterian Church. There was a man standing by the church gesturing toward the very figure that was the object of our attention. Drawn by the man's enthusiasm and obvious expertise, we approached to hear him addressing a group of tourists. The speaker turned out to be Ronn Shaffer, parishioner and noted historian of Old Pine. This knowledgeable man was able to shed a good deal of light on the tall dark figure that had recently been sculpted by Roger Wing.

What Mr. Shaffer told us of the sculpture is a tale of the interaction of human and natural forces. The cemetery fence was constructed in 1835, and coexisted peacefully with the Norway maple that was planted beside it in the early 1900's. But as the tree grew, its roots came to impinge on the base of the fence, pushing the fence to tilt precariously over the sidewalk outside the cemetery. The tree and the fence were at odds. According to Morris Arboretum experts who were called in to help arbitrate the tree vs. fence conflict, the maple had outlived its normal life-expectancy. This assessment provided rationale for ending the maple's life, thereby stopping the growth of its troublesome roots. The tree was hewn to a height of a sixteen foot stump. This stump would be put to two purposes. The first purpose is functional as the tree is tethered to the fence by steel cable to support the leaning structure. The dead tree has thereby been commissioned to uphold the fence it threatened to knock down while it was living. The second purpose is artistic.

Through the ministrations of sculptor Roger Wing, the large tree stump also serves as both pedestal for and figure of George Duffield, the pastor who served this historic church in the Revolutionary War era. Although the George Duffield statue is a recent convert from the plant kingdom, having been a living Norway maple tree until late 2015, the figure bears the determined demeanor of colonial-era piety. The sculpture depicts him in his role as chaplain of the Continental Army, addressing words of inspiration to the troops on the battlefield. George Duffield was a great proponent of the revolution against British tyranny. His emotional sermons inspired parishioners to join the fight and gave Old Pine the nickname "Church of the Patriots."

Duffield graduated the College of New Jersey (which would later become Princeton University) in 1752. He became an ordained Presbyterian minister and served congregations in central Pennsylvania before being called to the Pine Street Presbyterian church in 1771 when the country was on the verge of revolution. Emotions were high. The Presbyterian church was embroiled in an internal conflict between proponents of what was known as the New Side and those adherents to the Old Side. Duffield received a strongly mixed welcome. Though the majority of the congregation was on the New Side as was Duffield, there was a substantial number of dissenting Old-Siders some of whom took it upon themselves to lock the new New Side preacher out of the church on his arrival. The dispute took on a physical aspect as a group of New Side congregants introduced George Duffield to his new pastoral position in a highly unorthodox manner. His boosters literally boosted him into the church through the window.

In the right hand of the Duffield figure is a bible. It is not surprising for a pastor to be holding a bible. But it is particularly appropriate for George Duffield to be depicted with bible in hand, for he had a hand in editing the Aitken Bible, the first American bible. It was printed under the authority of the Continental Congress in 1782 when the wartime ban on British imports had caused a shortage of bibles in the colonies along with other goods. This was all part of the struggle that gave rise to the United States.

So many intervening wars have distanced the American psyche from the American Revolution. But that was the war that made it all possible. Patriotism has taken on many faces and many guises, but the face of George Duffield connects us to the very origin of American patriotism. His face reflects the travail involved in birthing a nation, the outrage that spurs revolution.

Roger Wing has captured that look of "We're mad as hell and we're not going to take it anymore!" Colonial patriotism was dedication to the overthrow of tyranny. This is the original American patriotism that has slipped off into history. Yet we can see it today in the face of George Duffield and the attitude of the figure that inclines forward with unflinching determination. His left hand thrusts upward and outward two fingers in a gesture that is clearly not a peace sign. George Duffield means business, and the business is creation of a nation.

The business of creating a wood sculpture is another matter, but one that requires great determination as well. Just as the competition between tree and fence is a reflection on the man-nature struggle, so is the travail of the wood sculptor. Roger Wing has noted, "I am trying to exert my will and create the form that I imagined, but the tree is always pushing back." Wing is aware of his connection to the beginnings of American sculpture. In the Fall 2009 issue of SVJ, there was mention of William Rush, called by the Philadelphia Gazette, "the father of American Sculpture." Rush's medium was wood. He fashioned the wood figures of *Comedy* and *Tragedy* displayed at the Chestnut Street Theater in the early 1800's as well as *Water Nymph and Bittern,* the first publicly funded public fountain in United States. Wood was the preferred sculpture medium in this country in the early nineteenth century, for marble was rare and wood plentiful. Bronze has become the prevalent statuary substance. But there remain sculptors like Roger Wing who, by their choice of material, go back to the roots of American sculpture. Wing is fully aware of the history of wood-carving in Philadelphia, and of William Rush who cut his sculptural teeth as a carver of ships' figureheads. Rush went on to carve wood statuary figures painted to resemble marble for public display. Wing remarked, "I feel like I am kind of going in reverse - I am carving our founding fathers in wood, and maybe I'll end up carving ship's figureheads."

We don't expect there will be much call for Mr. Wing's services from the ship-building industry. Transportation and art have changed immeasurably since the days of William Rush. Religion and politics have changed from the time of George Duffield. We remain at sea in these areas. The waters are rough and it's hard to navigate when you don't know what lies beyond the horizon. But a look back with the help of a wood sculptor and an historian may help us get our bearings.

References:
http://hiddencityphila.org/2015/11/spiritual-firebrand-of-the-revolutionary-war-immortalized-in-wood
http://articles.philly.com/2015-10-31/news/67883047_1_duffield-wood-battlefield
https://en.wikipedia.org/wiki/George_Duffield_(Reverend)
https://en.wikipedia.org/wiki/Robert_Aitken_%28publisher%29
http://www.thisday.pcahistory.org/tag/rev-george-duffield-1732-1790

THE FATHER OF MODERN POETRY

by Joe Tyson

Heinrich Heine was born in Dusseldorf's Jewish ghetto on December 13, 1797 to Peira Van Geldern Heine, the orphan of a physician, and small tradesman Samson Heine.

Little Harry's parents sent him to Jewish and Christian schools. His ambivalence toward both cultures made him feel like a foreigner in his own land. Local Christian bullies taunted him. It didn't help that the local junkman constantly shouted at his donkey, named "Harry."

Heine received good first impressions of the French. While Napoleon's soldiers were quartered in Dusseldorf, his father's store prospered. The Emperor's philo-Semitic policies encouraged optimism among Jews desiring to assimilate into German society. These hopes were dashed by the reaction following the Congress of Vienna. In his student years Heine cherished the notion of a joint German-Jewish venture to unite Germany's far-flung duchies by peaceful negotiation, and liberalize Europe along French lines. Bitter experience caused him to abandon this pipe dream, though he continued to regard France as a source of progressive ideals.

As an adolescent Heinrich demonstrated facility with language and scathing wit. However, his literary gifts were accompanied by impracticality. Although he detested business, Samson Heine arranged for him to work as a bank clerk trainee in Frankfurt. Seventeen-year-old Harry's duties as a scrivener were merely tiresome. What happened on Sundays traumatized him. Dusseldorf did not overtly persecute Jews. However, Frankfurt police still observed the medieval custom of locking all Jews inside the overcrowded Jewish quarter from dawn to dusk on Sundays. Young Heine felt unwanted and alienated.

By dint of hard work and extraordinary business acumen Heinrich's paternal Uncle Salomon had become one of Hamburg's wealthiest bankers. Relations between uncle and nephew were often strained. A hard-headed entrepreneur, Salomon never appreciated belles-lettres. For his part, Heinrich usually showed more insolence than gratitude. Heine's partisans have exaggerated Uncle Salomon's "stinginess." He not only set up his ungrateful nephew in business, but paid for his college education, law school tuition, and most living expenses until age thirty. After "Luftmensch" Heinrich moved to Paris he frequently sent importuning letters to his rich uncle and received substantial donations by return post. Following Salomon's death, his son Karl paid Heinrich an annual pension of 4,800 francs, which he later increased to 8,000. Nevertheless, Heine's disciples fault his affluent Hamburg relations for being "philistines," declining to send money during certain emergencies, and for burning those passages from the poet's unpublished memoirs which libeled them.

In 1818 Uncle Salomon purchased a retail clothing store in Hamburg for Heinrich. Due his nephew's lethargy it folded within a year, prompting Salomon to write him off as "an empty-headed idler." To escape from the grind of retail trade, Harry sought solace in the arms of prostitutes, and soon contracted venereal disease.

Heinrich Heine aspired to be a poet, even though he realized that an inordinately high number of bards died in almshouses of consumption. Literary magazines had already printed many of his poems. In 1821 he published a collection of romantic poetry entitled Gedichte. His Book of Songs followed in 1827.

In 1819 Heine prevailed upon Uncle Salomon to subsidize legal studies. That year he attended Bonn University, where he met philosophers Hegel and Schlegel, then subsequently transferred to the universities of Gottingen and Berlin. Though ostensibly pursuing a law degree, Harry mainly elected courses in the humanities. He enjoyed college life, while disapproving of nationalistic fraternities at Gottingen. In Heine's mind those militant secret societies were breeding grounds for chauvinism, a mind-set incompatible with Gottingen's liberal arts tradition. Fraternity brothers wrongly imagined that they glorified the Vaterland by despising Jews.

University friends appreciated Heine's sense of humor. He joked that his closet-sized apartment was so small that he had to leave before his roommate could enter. According to legend a ghost walked through Gottingen's campus at night along Pandect Lane. Harry quipped that this spirit must have been a student who had died from boredom. His readings of Voltaire and the French encyclopedists turned him into an agnostic.

Because Jews could not practice law in Germany, Heine converted to Protestantism in 1825. This move did not make him socially acceptable. The King of Bavaria rejected his application for a professorship at Munich University. No law firm hired him. Heine's ambiguous status as a baptized Jew intensified his angst. The conversion caused Jews to reject him, but didn't win approval from gentiles. In December, 1825 he advised Jewish friend Moses Moser not to convert.

In 1828 Baron Cotta, publisher of Munich's Political Annals Magazine, offered Heine a position as editor. He accepted, but threw this sinecure away within a year because political journalism cramped his imagination. Heine returned to his parents' new residence in Luneburg, which he dubbed "the capital of tedium." It was a cold and unfriendly place where he "made the acquaintance only of trees."

Meanwhile Heine signed up with literary agent and publisher Julius Campe. Biographer Lewis Browne observed that their relationship refuted age-old stereotypes, in that shrewd gentile Campe outsmarted naive Jewish Heine at every turn. With Campe's help Heine published Travel Pictures, a popular book of essays which disseminated liberal views with cynical humor. Unfortunately, his satirical jibes did not go unnoticed by the Prussian Bureau of Censorship, which promptly banned it. Heine's 12th chapter particularly rankled them.

> "The German censors of the press......
> ....
> .... blockheads!.......................
> ...."

As a leading member of The Young German Movement Heine believed that Germany could lead the way toward European emancipation of workingmen, Jews, rural peasants, and the press. Young Germans championed such progressive causes as free speech, separation of church and state, equal rights for women, and the overthrow of hereditary noblemen.

Heine befriended fellow radicals Ludwig Borne, Karl Marx, Friedrich Engels, and Ferdinand Lassalle. His writings reflected a cosmopolitan and anti-aristocratic bent. He railed against

> "nobles who have learned nothing beyond
> horse-trading, card-sharping, drinking feats,
> and similar stupid rascally accomplishments."

He referred to castles as "lodging houses for blackguards," knights as "ass-drivers," ladies in waiting as "common wenches," and monarchical governments as "puppet comedies." He despised nationalists, whom he described as "false patriots whose love of the Fatherland consists of nothing but an insane hatred of foreigners and neighbors, notably France." He worried about the underlying barbarism of German racists. They wanted

> "the old stone gods (to) rise from their long-forgotten ruins... (so that) Thor, leaping to life with his giant hammer (could) crush the Gothic cathedrals!"

Heine predicted that socialism would eventually defeat these "Teutomaniacs" in a deadly struggle. His words prophesy the National Socialist movement.

> "A drama will be enacted in Germany by the side of which the French Revolution will seem like an innocent idyll."

In 1829 the restless Heine moved to Potsdam and supported himself by writing articles. He withdrew from such friends as Christian Sethe, Ludwig Borne, and Rahel von Varnhagen in order to concentrate on writing. The solitary poet compared himself to

> "Robinson Crusoe on (an) island... For company I had only the statues in the Gardens of Sancouci. I kept from all contact with the outer world, and if anyone so much as brushed against me in the street I felt an uneasy sensation. I had a profound horror of such encounters... like that which... wandering... spirits of the dead feel when ... they meet a living man..."

Heine's periodic bouts of introversion stemmed from a combination of shyness, ambivalence about his Jewishness, and an obsessive desire to write without interruption.

The poet suffered from a variety of neuroses, including anxiety, melancholia, hypochondria, obsessive-compulsive behavior, and oversensitivity to noise. Harsh criticisms could reduce him to tears. The ticking of clocks bothered him abnormally. He could not have any timepiece in his study or bedroom, and would often ask guests to put their watches in a drawer. In Paris the piano practicing of girls in a nearby apartment drove him to distraction.

A trip to England in September, 1827 triggered a phobic response. The poet saw one huge bedlam, a horrifying phantasmagoria, marked by

> "colossal uniformity, machine-like movement
> …. shrillness… a stone forest of houses…
> between … surging stream(s) of living human
> faces…"

Florid John Bulls and their cocksure female counterparts frightened him. "Send a philosopher to London, but… not a poet!"17 he exclaimed.

Heine's newspaper and magazine articles consisted mainly of social criticism. Ernst Pawel observed Heine always knew what he opposed, "but seldom what he (was) for." Nietszche praised Heine for "divine malice," but others have accused him of being "negative"—a cynical pessimist rather than architect of reforms. No political system ever satisfied him.

In Letters from Berlin (1822) and Travel Pictures (1827) Heine dealt more with sharply expressed opinions than facts. His poison pen soon got him into trouble. Anti-Semitic playwright Count von Platen lampooned him as "the Pindar of Benjamin's tribe… Petrarch of the Feast of Booths… baptized Heine… pride of the synagogue…". Those spiteful taunts struck a nerve. Admitting that he was "but a novice in Christian love," Heine lashed back at Platen by outing him as a homosexual. An attack on ex-friend Ludwig Borne displeased many left-leaning readers.

Heine's celebrations of French Revolution ideals put him in bad odor with Prussian authorities. His unrestrained diatribe against Count von Platen attracted more unwanted attention from them. Heine complained: "now I've been forbidden to write!"

Unable to bear Germany's oppressive atmosphere any longer, thirty-three-year-old Heine emigrated to Paris in April, 1831. He became a boulevardier at once, making friends with Balzac, Beranger, George Sand, Gerard de Nerval, Hippolyte Taine, Theophile Gautier, Alexander Dumas, Giacomo Meyerbeer, Hector Berlioz, and Franz Liszt. French writer Philibert Audebrand remembered walking past Frascatti's Restaurant with Dr. Heller of the French Academy when the latter halted in his tracks, gestured toward Heine seated at a table, and excitedly whispered: "there is the wittiest man in Europe!"

At the urging of irrepressible utopian Prosper Enfantin, Heine joined the St. Simonists. This politico-philosophical society advocated communal living and secular humanism. Count St. Simon (Claude Henri De Rouvroy) not only touted equality, fraternity, and liberty, but sharing of goods, universal suffrage, public education, meritocracy, women's liberation, and rule by councils of artists, poets, and scientists. St. Simon's unbounded optimism led him to believe that modern technology would redistribute wealth, raising everyone's standard of living. Though Heine did not swallow St. Simonism whole, he began to view himself as an internationalist. In a letter to his friend Alfred Meissner he wrote:

> "I have this in common with all other
> artists; I do not write for the moment
> but for centuries, not for a country but
> for the world, not for a party, but for
> humanity."

Heine agreed with St. Simonist visionaries that poetic intuition should not be lightly dismissed, asserting: "the poet's heart is the center of the world." Being a German Jew living in France he fancied himself as a conciliator between the two nations: "the one writer sufficiently conversant with both cultures to interpret one to the other," and defuse mutual distrust. Of course, neither country ever recognized him as the "Jewish middleman" to broker peace through meaningful compromise. He had to satisfy his longing for rapprochement on a small scale by elucidating German culture to the French in works such as The Romantic School (1833) and History of Religion and Philosophy in Germany (1835.)

Heine's poem "This and That Side of the Rhine" summarized his views.

> "Wild caresses, tender throes,
>   Toying with a burning rose,
>   Fragrant fetor, pretty lies,
>   Raw lust in a noble guise,
>   Love's glad arts in any wise—
>   Ah, you French have mastered those!
>
> But we Germans bow to none
>   When there's hating to be done.
>   German hate! It swells and spills
>   From the soul in giant rills,
>   And its poison overfills
>   Even Heidelberg's great tun."

Despite Heine's love for France, his devotion to Germany would not permit him to become a French citizen.

Besides gallivanting through salons with Gautier, Liszt, and Taine, Heine toured Paris's demimonde. In his travels among prostitutes and serving maids of easy virtue, he met shop girl Mathilde Cresentia Eugenie Mirat, a gay little Parisienne who laughed often and loved to sing, but never attended school. Heine became obsessed with her. They broke up numerous times, only to reconcile. One day, when some students in a café flirted with her, the enraged poet slapped their ringleader's face and challenged him to a duel (which never occurred.) In September, 1841 Heine announced his marriage to Mathilde by writing to his sister Charlotte:

> "on the 31st of August I married Mathilde...
> with whom I have previously quarreled daily
> for more than six years."

He told friend Caroline Jaubert that she aimed a pistol at him during the wedding ceremony. Heine in-formed Alexander Weill that he had to buy Mathilde from an aunt for 3,000 francs. He claimed to have spent another 10,000 on tutors in an effort to teach her to read and write. Even after those expenditures she did not realize her husband was a Jew, and could not read his literary works. Heine asserted that Mathilde believed him when he told her that Jesus Christ was Archbishop of Paris. Ernst Pawel described Mathilde as

> "a tough, cantankerous and shamelessly
> egotistical woman.... Quite possibly she saw
> in him little more than a meal ticket... She may
> have been genuinely fond of him in her own way,
> though she definitely fussed a great deal more
> about a sick parrot than... sick husband."

In spite of her faults, Heine sincerely loved Mathilde -- although that did not prevent him from engaging in some infidelities between 1842 and 1844. He diligently provided for her material needs, and put up with a great deal of nonsense. Letters to his mother and sister usually showed Mathilde in a favorable light. However, Heine wrote a short dialogue in verse between mother and son having dinner, which illustrated his own inclination to change the subject when pressed for information about Mathilde. The mother asked:

"My darling child, in your foreign home
Are you carefully served and tended?
Does your wife understand how to keep house?
Are your shirts and stockings mended?"

The son evades these questions by replying:

"Dear little mother, this fish is good,
But fish is a risky diet;
You so easily choke on a bone if you speak;
Just leave me a moment in quiet."

During long absences—such as his 1843 trip to Germany—Heine missed Mathilde, and experienced fits of deep mistrust. He recalled that it had not been very difficult, as a total stranger, to seduce her after their first meeting in 1834. Thus, Heine worried that she would cheat on him. From Hamburg the possessive husband wrote:

"I am thinking only of you, my dear
Nonotte.... do not forget that my eyes
are always upon you. I know everything
you do, and what I don't know I shall
learn later."

In spite of his entreaties for letters, she only dashed off a few short notes in six weeks. He scolded her for neglecting him.

"I am exceedingly angry with you, and
when I arrive I shall give you only
five hundred kisses, instead of a
thousand!"

Heinrich knew Karl and Jenny Marx personally and seems to have first coined the expression "Marxist platitude."

Marx dismissed him as "one of those queer fowl called poets."
Between 1844 and 1845 Heine visited the Marxes often at
their apartment in Rue Vanneau. On one occasion their baby
daughter Jennychen suffered from such severe cramps that
they feared for her life. Heine coolly took charge, instructing
Mrs. Marx to give the infant a warm bath, which immediately
stabilized her condition. The thankful couple credited him
with saving Jennychen's life.

Heine favored freedom of the press and social programs for the downtrodden, however his enthusiasm for the
masses waned after 1840. The mobs of Paris cheered mass
executions in 1789. While he loathed aristocratic cads, Heine
also "closed his ears to the shouting of the Marseillaise." Most
common people were brutal illiterates, who let unscrupulous
demagogues entice them with bread, circuses, and conspiracy
theories. In "Lamentations" he slammed the United States,
world capital of slavery, as "... America the Free, ... that Freedom stable where all the boors live equally...". In contrast to
Friedrich Engels, Ludwig Borne, and Ferdinand Lassalle,
Heine "did not like to fraternize with sweaty workers and
refused to address them as comrades." Communist agitator
and tailor Wilhelm Weitling offended the poet by not removing his hat when addressing him. Anticipating Orwell
and Huxley, Heine envisioned a "proletarian paradise" with
abominable popular culture.

> "With their horny hands they will heartlessly
> smash the marble statues of beauty so dear
> to my heart...They will cut down my grove of
> laurels and plant potatoes in their stead. They
> will tear from ... the social order ...
> lilies that toil not or spin... My Book of Songs
> will be used to ... wrap coffee or snuff
> for ... old women of the future."

Those snobbish premonitions struck a resonant chord with King Louis-Phillipe, who awarded the erstwhile revolutionary a pension. German newspapers that employed Heine as a columnist did not find out about this French subsidy until the collapse of Louis's regime during the Revolution of 1848. The Allgemeine Zeitung and other papers indignantly dropped him for being a propagandist on France's payroll. Heine pleaded that Louis-Phillipe and his minister Francois Guizot had simply given him "alms." He applied for this hand-out "after the Bundestag's ... deplorable decrees ... which tried to ruin me financially because I was...choir leader of Young Germany."

His fellow pensioners included

> "exiles from every quarter of the globe,
> refugees from Greece, Santo Domingo, Armenia,
> Poland... Barons and princes... are among them,
> generals, ex-ministers, even priests, forming as it
> were, an aristocracy of poverty."

But Heine's credibility in Germany evaporated overnight. None of his arguments swayed editors, who blackballed him.

In 1832 Heine experienced intermittent numbness in the fingers of his left hand. Five years later the thirty-nine-year-old poet wrote his friend J. H. Detmold:

> "My left hand is getting thinner and
> thinner and is withering away
> perceptibly."

He soon lost control of his left eyelid and began to hobble around on crutches. By 1848 Heine's vision deteriorated and he could not walk. The bedridden poet spoke of being confined to a

"mattress-tomb without repose, death without the
privileges of the dead, who are not required to spend
money or write letters."

His last excursion under his own power took place
in May, 1848. With superhuman effort he dragged himself
to The Louvre, but collapsed beneath the statue of Venus de
Milo.

"At her feet I lay for a long time and wept...
the blessed goddess of beauty... looked
down on me with mingled compassion and
desolation, seeming to say: 'dost thou not
see I have no arms, and therefore cannot
help thee?' ..."

Shortly thereafter his friend Alfred Meissner asked if
he'd like to go anywhere. Heine answered "to St. Sulpice."
Meissner expressed surprise that an agnostic would want to
go to church. The poet retorted: "where else should one go
with crutches?"

Due to dissipations in Hamburg thirty years earlier,
Heine now suffered the ravages of tertiary syphilis. He called
his condition "spine rot," declaring "I have suffered more
tortures than the Spanish Inquisition could invent." In a
letter to Ferdinand Lasalle he wrote:

"I kiss, but feel nothing. My palate and ... part
of my tongue are also touched and everything I
eat tastes like earth."

To his brother Max he announced: "the advance
guard of decrepitude has taken up its stand. My youth is
gone...".

During the final six years of his life Heine required
custodial nursing care. His sister Charlotte referred in a

letter to her brother's "shriveled body with … lifeless legs," and how his nurse would carry him like a grotesque baby from couch to bed. She had to rub his open bed sores with paregoric salve daily. Heine jested that opium was the only "religion" that consoled him. He preferred opium-soaked poultices to Christian preaching, since "the relief is prompter." Sneezes, coughs, and yawns brought excruciating torment.

> "These yawns are unbearable. I wish I
> were dead, or else a healthy fellow who
> no longer needs enemas."

For amusement, house-bound Heine sometimes borrowed his wife's binoculars to view Parisian street scenes. In 1854 he wrote:

> "with incredible pleasure (I) watched a
> pastry baker offer his wares to two ladies in
> crinolines and a little dog standing on three
> legs by a tree next to them, relieving himself.
> At that point I put away the binoculars. I didn't
> want to see any more because I envied the dog."

Many recognize Heine as the father of black humor. During his protracted illness he spoke himself as "a decomposing corpse," ruefully adding that

> "they took my measurements long ago for the
> coffin and … obituary."

He now realized that there was an afterlife, since "I have survived my own death." Heine told visitors: "my constitution is worse than Prussia's."

Many German callers visited his apartment during The Paris World's Fair of 1855, prompting him to comment that he should be paid as one of the exposition's "sideshow exhibits." When his nurse lugged him into the living room on one occasion, he quipped: "do you see how they carry me about on their hands in Paris?" Guests politely inquired about his prospects. When one asked if his condition was curable, he replied: "yes, I shall die someday." Since he had wasted away to such an extent, Heine remarked that he would "have to apologize to the worms for offering them nothing but bones." Heine told friends who knew of his repugnance for noise that it distressed him "to hear death (constantly) sharpening his scythe." He sadly informed them: "one day you'll find the booth closed where the puppet show of my humor… entertained you."

Heine clung to a "worthless existence," noting that "the horrible thing is dying, not death." He compared himself to a bag of bones lying on a dock waiting through endless delays for his "voyage to eternity." To him time seemed like "a dreadful snail crawling at … sluggish pace."

In November, 1849 Heine grumbled about France's high cost of living to Julius Campe:

> "It's already expensive to live in Paris. But dying in
> Paris is infinitely more expensive. And to think that
> I could be hung for free in Germany…"

Heine groused about being unable to shed his Jewishness and become a "joyful Hellene." He cried that "no pagan gods would have done to a poet what … Jehovah did to me!" He portrayed himself as "a poor sick Jew," and God as

> "The Aristophanes of heaven (who) shows
> me, the little German so-called Aristophanes
> of earth, … how pitifully I lag behind him
> in humor and the making of colossal jokes."

Nevertheless, like his admirer Kierkegaard, Heine now handed his affairs over to God, and felt thankful that someone "upstairs" heard his "whimpering ..., especially after midnight." He depicted his sudden piety as "surprising to God," but insisted that he was still not a "pious lambkin." In fact, his new-found faith increased the pleasure of swearing.

> "Thank God I have a God again so that when the agony gets too bad I can let go of a few blasphemous curses. Atheists don't have that satisfaction."

Of course, he realized that his return to the fold had no effect on God.

> "The great white elephant of the King of Siam could not care less whether or not a little mouse in ... Rue d'Amsterdam believes in his grandeur and wisdom..."

At his wit's end on the eve of death in January, 1856, he wrote:

> "I am almost going out of my mind with rage, anguish, and impatience. I am going to complain to The Animal Protection League about a God who tortures me so cruelly."

When friends professed shock at his irreverence, he shot back: "God will forgive me—that's His trade."

Anxious about Mathilde's welfare, the shut-in poet continued to write. He published Romanzero, a volume of poetry in 1851, Confessions in 1853, and collections of poems in 1853 and 1854. Heine also arranged for a 4,800 franc annual stipend from his cousin Karl.

Mathilde did not reciprocate. Protesting that the smell of her husband's sickroom made her ill, she avoided it. Her laziness forced disabled Heinrich to pay for a nurse and cleaning lady, as well as a secretary for himself. Though she claimed to lack nursing skills, Heine noticed that Mathilde treated their pet cat with tender solicitude when he injured his paw after a fall. A compulsive shopper, she constantly bought clothing, knick-knacks, and anything made of linen, including curtains, table-cloths, bedding, etc. Her spending sprees continued even when funds and apartment space ran out. Because of

Heinrich Heine
by Marcellin-Gilbert Desboutin c. 1850

substantial weight gain due to gluttony, Mathilde continually required new finery, reasoning that she needed more elegant clothes to compensate for her fading looks.

Despite Heinrich's morbid aversion to noise, Mathilde purchased a parrot named "Cocotte," who squawked loudly at unpredictable intervals. When Mathilde's neurotic and slothful friend Pauline Rogue fell on hard times, she took her into the household. To Heine's chagrin Elise Arnault, the boisterous wife of a circus impresario, barged in almost daily. The dying poet wished Mathilde to remarry after his demise. Then "at least one man on earth… will regret my passing!"

Although Heine tried his best to put up with Mathilde's insufferable minions, she mistreated his own friends. When Alexander Weill commented one evening that the fish Mathilde just served emitted an unsavory odor, she threw the whole serving plate into his face. One day, Dr. Wertheimer urged Mathilde to provide better care for Heinrich. Before he could finish, she hauled off and punched him in the eye. The doctor left in a huff, abandoning Heine to the whims of Dr. Gruby, a proponent of strychnine, leeches, neck drilling, hot irons, and bloodletting. Though he preferred Wertheimer, Heine admitted that neither "quack" did him much good, noting that "all the people who died here this winter had medical attendance."

Heine had a rope loop above his bed to help him change positions. When Caroline Jaubert asked him the purpose of this device, he said:

> "a gymnastic invention, supposedly to help
> me exercise my right arm. But frankly,
> between you and me, I rather suspect
> it to be an invitation… to hang myself, a
> delicate hint from my doctor…"

For short time the Heines employed a comely and pleasant young nurse named Marietta, who delighted Heinrich. Jealous Mathilde fired Marietta and hired a churlish old crone as her replacement.

On June 19, 1855 an attractive young fan of Heine named Camille Selden called on him. Enchanted by the girl, "last flower of my mournful autumn," the poet begged her to visit again. Summoning all his strength he wrote this letter.

"My dear amiable and charming person,
I greatly regret having been able to see you but
for a few moments. You made an extremely
favorable impression, and I am longing for the
pleasure of seeing you again. If possible, come
tomorrow, or in any case, whenever time permits.
Announce yourself as last time. I am ready to
receive you at any hour. The best time for me
would be from 4 P.M. until as late as you want.
Despite my eye trouble I am writing you with
my own hand, because at the moment I don't
have a confidential secretary. I have lots of
trouble on my plate and am suffering a great deal.
I don't know why your kind sympathy seems to do
me so much good and why I want to imagine,
superstitious as I am, that a good fairy is
visiting me in a sad hour. It was the right hour.
Or are you a bad fairy? I must find out soon."

Mathilde detested Miss Selden and would not speak to her. Nevertheless, Camille came regularly to cheer up dying Heinrich. To her he wrote:

"I am now merely a ghost.... I look
forward to seeing you again, fine
Mouche de mon ame... loveliest of
muskrats... soft like an angora cat. I
am still in a bad state, constant cramps
and anger... A dead man thirsting for
the greatest of life's pleasures..."

Camille last visited him on Valentine's Day, 1856, three days before his death. "At last you have come!" he exclaimed, and wept at the thought of being "a cadaver in love."

Heine once said "poetry is my best friend." The writing obsession stayed with him to the very end. Despite acute suffering he habitually scribbled sentences and phrases. When nurse Catherine Bourlois chided him for writing six hours straight in February, 1856, he cried: "I only have four more days to work!" On his deathbed a few days later he wanted to write, but was too sick. Catherine tried to comfort him, saying: "when you stop throwing up, you'll write." Faintly but distinctly he sighed: "I'm dying." He then kept repeating "I'm lost." Suddenly, at 4 A.M. he seemed to rally. In a hoarse voice he panted: "write—write! Paper... pencil," then became delirious. Heinrich Heine died at 5 A.M. on 2/17/1856.

One of Heine's poems related the tale of a crusader for freedom married to a slattern.

> "At six in the morning he was hanged
>   At seven lowered into the grave;
>   She, however, by eight o'clock
>   Already drank red wine and laughed."

Mathilde did not attend Heinrich's funeral at Montmartre Cemetery. No less an authority than Karl Marx declared her guilty of having an adulterous affair during Heine's final years. With the assistance of Henri Julia and an unscrupulous lawyer, Mathilde managed to support herself until 1883 by selling her late husband's manuscripts to the highest bidders. She and Julia allegedly sold some of Heine's papers to one of his male cousins, knowing full well that he intended to burn them.

Despite the grievous travail he endured during the last eight years of his life, Heinrich Heine never lost his sense of humor. He struck admirers as being ahead of his time. Many still revere him as Europe's first modern intellectual.

A POET OF THE SACRED:
DANIEL ABDAL HAYY-MOORE

by Robert Zaller

I had a nodding acquaintance with the poet Daniel Abdal Hayy-Moore, but some nods are more significant than others. I encountered him at venues shortly after he moved to Philadelphia in 1990, and liked what I heard of his work. We got no closer than that, but over the years we developed a fellow acknowledgment. I knew Daniel had been part of the Beat poetry scene in the Sixties and that he had converted to Sufism thereafter, adding an adopted Muslim name to his given one. I knew, too, that he was immensely prolific, producing a tome of verse or more each year under his own imprint, The Ecstatic Exchange. This seemed grounds for a certain wariness, since good poetry rarely grows in clusters, and self-published work, especially in quantity, suggests a certain isolation. But it was also true that Daniel was unfailingly cordial and unprepossessing; there was nothing of the neglected genius about him. He was simply a man who had gone his own idiosyncratic way. He wasn't indifferent to recognition—no serious artist conscious of his gifts is—but he knew the path he had chosen, of producing a grand spiritual autobiography in verse while practicing a faith alien to the experience of most of his fellow countrymen—was not conducive to conventional success. Daniel did have some outreach in the American Muslim community, but here, too, he was appealing to a group that, like other minorities, had mostly practical concerns, and no ready niche for someone who, coming up through the Berkeley of Allen Ginsberg and Lawrence Ferlinghetti, had pitched on an esoteric branch of Islam via a brief but critical immersion in Tantric Buddhism.

The body of Daniel's work would probably have remained largely unknown to me too had he not asked me to review one of his volumes. The one I chose was *Stretched Out* on *Amethysts,* a title that (like The Ecstatic Exchange) seemed a little over the top to me, but actually referred to a treatment Daniel had taken for back pain. It was typical of Daniel to see the spiritual and the corporal as a single continuum, a faculty particularly difficult to cultivate in American culture but one which served him in good stead during his long final illness.

The two hundred odd pages of *Amethysts* were a revelation to me. The poems were free-ranging, and daring in their honesty; they both acknowledged the quotidian and risked the sublime. Like Daniel's other volumes, the poems were arranged chronologically, as if part of a running poetic diary, and they encompassed only a period of several months. When I looked at the number of previous volumes listed opposite the title page, I realized I was dealing with a significant if not major body of work. A few hundred poems would constitute the lifetime achievement of most poets, and a dozen in an anthology might suffice to make a reputation. But here was a poet whose output was clearly in the thousands, and there was no reason to believe that the caliber of what I'd read was exceptional to the whole—as, in fact, it wasn't.

Daniel's earliest work had been published by Ferlinghetti's City Lights Press, and a later volume was issued by an academic publisher, Syracuse, but it was clear to him once his vocation had fully settled in that no commercial outlet could be a catchment for his work. Most poets are content to winnow their work for publication, choosing from among the best or more representative of it to fit what conventionally makes for a volume of poetry, and most are happy to have a handful of such volumes represent a career. Daniel's project was different, a spiritual autobiography that attended to the gift of every day. Self-publication was the only practical answer to the problem, if the totality of his work was to appear as he wished. He saw it as a seamless integument, which to have cut it at any point would have vitiated the integrity of the whole.

Daniel's body of work—and it includes theater, art, and music as well as his writing—deserves a full-length study, and I can offer only a modest introduction here. I will concentrate on a single volume of his poetry, *Salt Prayers,* which I choose for no better (or worse) reason than that its spare title attracted me. The book covers a single five-month period of Daniel's late fifties, dated May 29 – October 24, 1998, during which he produced ninety poems covering 209 pages. I'll begin with one of the first of them, typical of the group as a whole in its wide embrace of subject matter though freer than most in its use of emphasis. It's called by its first full phrase:

Surprise! Here we are, still alive, under the
shadow of the great arch. How it

curves above us! The highest arc of it lost in blue clouds,
lost in white sky! It soars from somewhere behind us to
somewhere off in front! . . .
. . . .
   "Surprise! Here we are, still alive,
under the shadow of the great arch! Formed from
fists of dust and mud, inflated to full size with
spirit, destined to be broken-hearted, weighed
down, shoulders made expressly for
 burdens.

Today our hands are in our sleeves, gesturing and pointing!
Tomorrow the
sleeves will be all that remain, fluttering free!
Our coats will stand on their own and
 blow in the breeze!

Our pain will be released."
        ("Surprise! Here We Are, Still Alive")

The main body of the poem uses neither italics nor (with one exception) exclamation points. The italics emphasize quoted speech, and the 'speakers' of these lines are eyes that speak with "glances"—that is, the bodily testimony of perishing, organic creation rather than personalized consciousness. The poem's 'surprise' is the moment to moment discovery that life persists at all, its sole guarantee being the "great arch" that encloses it. Even this may be illusory, since only the shadow of the arch is visible—that is, its existence is inferential—and the shadow itself is incomplete, since the bridge of the arch is lost in a dimension itself unreal, "blue" clouds above a "white" sky. In short, life has no true guarantee at all, and the exclamation points indicate a hectic anxiety, the uncertain miracle of the self's moment to moment continuity.

The italicized passage, returning to the initial invocation of "surprise," is the concluding section of the poem. The "we" who are its subject are described as compounded of dust and mud, combatively tensed as "fists" but also inflated by something called "spirit," which results in shoulders built for burdens, and hearts made for breaking. These images suggest a somatic progression from the small, bunched ego of the infant to the full-scale body of the adult whose purposes are not its own, since it is "destined" and "made expressly" for duty and suffering—an animal that endures and feels, but cannot freely act.

The futility of human consciousness—i.e., its inability to act in such a way as to alter its circumstances and its fate—is indicated by the image of the sleeved hands, which 'gesture' and 'point' much as a small child does, but reach in the last analysis at nothing. This image serves to connect us with the ultimate futility of death: our empty sleeves 'survive' us, ironically fluttering "free" not in the sense of any will or capacity but merely to signify a release from pain that is extinction's sole reward.

"Surprise!" clearly suggests an unsparingly tragic vision of life, its despair only heightened by the poem's surreal touches and mock-comedic diction.

Only a day later—but several poems on—Daniel rings a change on the notion of the indignities of our corporal condition, and its implication for human relationships:

I sleep alone. I have for years.
I snore. I twitch, and out my rear
come sulfurous fumes no
mortal can endure.
I get up in the night to pee, once or twice,
throw off bedclothes, shuffle to the toilet.

My advice,
to grow in deep affection with your spouse:
sleep at the other end of the house.
                            ("I Sleep Alone")

This appears to be a poem of alienation—from one-self, from another—but it makes a sharp swerve: "Then meet with spouse to bacchanal in God's / Pleasure Dome, there feast, make joy, / embellish home with sensual ecstasy's / piping, the organ blowing its stack!" From the body at its unloveliest emerges the sacred animal to rejoice in the capacity for union and delight. "I Sleep Alone" sounds the full human register, asserting the essential rhythms of a long marriage and the spaces it needs for the self. It is wry and funny and wise, and in the end affirmative. The satisfied lover goes off again at the end "to snore" and perhaps to leave his wife to do the same, for privacy is the precondition of intimacy, and what one knows about others depends, too, on what one refrains from knowing—and revealing. There's a third party to the poem, too, namely the God in whose "Pleasure Dome" the lovers disport, and who wisely keeps his own counsel too: "God / holding His secrets back for a time, waiting for / the ripe moment to spring them, out of // bland even boring darkness" ("Cherry Tree, Apple Tree, Pear Tree, Quince").

The journey to the other that is the quest of love, then, is a pattern of the individual's path toward the supreme Other. We intuit the divine in our solitude, "staring out these human eyes of [ours] at a / universe not of [our] making" and offering "Salt prayers" to "that / Unseen Presence that is never absent, / that Absence never far from us." We know, instinctively, that the world we seem "momentarily trapped in" is, in moments of illumination or rapt contemplation, a transparency through which we may perceive God and feel ourselves perceived by him ("If I Were Trapped inside a Bottle"). Such moments are always available but, equally, they are rare. Truth, then, is not difficult to grasp beyond the quotidian, but it is difficult to hold. God, who is perfect intelligibility, is not the mystery of the world; rather, that mystery is the dark weave of matter that conceals the light, and the darkness in ourselves—somehow necessary, the cost and condition of creation—that deflects it. As in Daniel's image of the great arch, we live in shadow. But the light is not truly hidden; we must simply find means to reveal it, and that process is called living.

Daniel's poetry exhibits a lively appreciation of the world in its beauty, its diversity, and its pleasures. In the end, though, it is for him the medium through which we pursue the divine. This is a paradox, because the world is also a source of distraction, a puzzle palace that leads to dead ends. But, just as Daniel sees marriage as a mode of separation that leads to ecstatic union, so for him the embrace of the world, the openness to experience, is the condition of divine en-counter. That embrace cannot be indiscriminate, however, and it is only through learning the world's snares and pitfalls that we can find a proper place in it.

The most fateful of those snares, Daniel suggests, is the self. When he evokes the ignominy of the physical—his snoring, his farting, his glum humors and the assorted indignities of aging—he is not merely ridiculing himself, but practicing a kind of discipline, an *askesis* for putting the self in its place. Daniel deals directly with the problem in "Don't Look at Me!", which slangily evokes the old myths of Narcissus and Medusa:

the self,
one look and you're
hooked,

unhook yourself,
don't look.

The twist of language suggests the process we necessarily undergo in freeing ourselves from fatal preoccupation with the self. "Don't look," the poem instructs us, but it's already too late, because like Narcissus we've already done so: the experience is inevitable. The only solution is to "unhook" oneself; only then may the original injunction be obeyed. To do this, however, the self and its consequences must be confronted in all their unloveliness and ultimate absurdity:

I should eat grass,
mangy, goggle-eyed,
mad-brained, watch me
rise up like fart-mist over a swamp,
watch me
bubble up over a metropolitan area,
ho! City of a great culture,
arms liquicious,
swamp-gas,

I can hurl bombs, I can snarl
indignant rage, watch me
launch ships, rockets, watch my
fingers on the trigger and the
snigger on my face, yowl of
global gargantuousity, howl of
halitosis folderol, I'm
comin' like a banshee over the rooftops,
Schickelgruper-faced,
the self in all its
glory.

These lines are a good sample of Daniel on a roll, flinging out neologisms ("liquicious," "gargantuousity," "Schickelgruper-faced") as he builds up an image of the self as both the farcical monster of a 1950s horror movie and the gaseously inflated image of our so-called common humanity. The swamp-self bubbles up over the image of our urban sprawl ("metropolitan area"), mockingly projected as the "City of a great culture." Feeding on the spurious energy this provides, the engorged self embarks on an orgy of destruction, in the service as always of a righteous indignation, until it reaches its orgiastic crest, "comin' like a banshee over the rooftops." At the same time, the face momentarily assumes a particularly notorious set of features. "Schickelgruper-faced" combines the evocation of Adolf Hitler's birth name, Schickelgruber, with the "group" fanaticism in which it so disastrously resulted. The self identifying itself not only as the vital node of being but as the source of social creation—the mass of selves that, subordinated to a single will, constitutes the false idea of the Nation—leads both to the human usurpation of the divine and the truly mindless destruction that is its consequence. Taken to its logical conclusion of its depravity, then, the self is the antithesis of the divine, the decreating force that, in our post-nuclear sublime, threatens to destroy the world, or at least its human component.

This is the condition to which we have lately given a name, the anthropocene, and which Daniel lived long enough together with the rest of us to envision—a state in which human activity roils the balance of nature and precipitates catastrophic ecological change. For Daniel, however, the answer to this problem would not lie in technology or social engineering, but, as he enjoins us (imperatively, but, as usual, wittily) to reject in ourselves any final standard of value, and to seek it in its proper place:

paint it white, tack on wings, it's still sod!

Don't waste time seeking self.

Seek God!

The use of rhyme here, as elsewhere in the poem (look, hook; trigger, snigger) signifies radical apposition. Painting ourselves as angels, as companions of God and faultless agents of his will—another act of human pre-sumption—will do no more than putting on horror masks; we are still "sod," and it is only in fully acknowledging this that can we can aspire to understand anything else.

The question is what our exacerbated human con-sciousness is for, and why the world seemingly requires it to fulfill any purpose that comes at such cost. The self has no value as such, Daniel insists, except as the means of its own transcendence. How is this to occur, though, especially in a being overwhelmingly preoccupied with its own existence and the delusions of grandeur it generates? Daniel addresses this question in the poem titled, "Without a Thought in My Head." The mind, when truly emptied—that is, when ex-hausted by the search for meaning and value, for the least sign of redemptive grace—confronts its own sense of isolation in an alien universe. This is contrasted with the 'contentment' of the cherry pit, a particularly humble form of life:

the cherry pit is contented with dulcet
cherry meat around it and the
 scant possibility it
just might one day become a
 cherry tree.

The cherry pit does not *know* it will become a cherry tree; it merely feels the sweet meat that grows around it ("dulcet" is a beautiful choice here), and intuits a further transformation it cannot fully conceive but that will fulfill its destiny. This is a kind of consciousness, imputed to organic matter but more limited than that of mind. If the pit could indeed conceive the tree as we do, as a solitary growth in a world of things in which it must take root and thrive and in which will it finally decay and perish, its contentment would presumably be less if at all. But the pit's world extends no further than the vision of the tree, and the tree is thus its *ne plus ultra,* its god. Man's more restless capacity is to think beyond the physical incarnation of self toward that which lies ineffably beyond it, for which a mind emptied of self and world—that is, in the trance-like state of negative capability that Keats suggested as the mental precondition of the poem—was necessary.

Daniel has already alerted us to the fact that it is not merely snoring that keeps him from his wife at night, but the unpredictable visits of the Muse. This sets the scene for a quasi-epiphanic experience:

my black cat's coming around the
 corner of my bed to see
what in the world has got my
 attention at 3 AM—

nothing in the world, Raven Silhouette,
but this itch to sing a poem
 under the brute
 indifferent sky

knowing One Alone listens Who's
in my heart
and has His Reasons to

listen as I

have my reasons to sing.

Daniel's poem has elements of both prayer and lament, without quite settling on either. It presents itself in the home-ly form of an "itch" to sing, an urge that seems to come from nowhere and to expend itself on nothing. At the same time, the poet affirms that the Deity not only hears but actively listens to the song. Even more confidently, he states that the "One Alone" is in his heart, so that nothing essentially separates them—except the poem itself, whose function, then, is to explore existential distance. That distance—the one between creator and created—of course ontologically exists, at least for those who accept theistic premises. It is normally postulated as the result of divine agency, and thus as constituted on God's terms. The poem, however, suggests that this space is actually open and dynamic, and can be acted upon by both parties; that, indeed, it is precisely in this that man's free will consists. The poet sings for reasons of his own, necessary or sufficient to him, and God (it is posited) listens for reasons personal to him as well. What passes between God and man in this exchange is thus respect, the respect of difference. The poet makes the sign of his speaking and God the sign of his listening, and this is the token of their exchange.

Again and again in Daniel's poetry, the distance between divine perfection and human perception is probed, tested, personalized. This entails an accordion-like adjustment of focus between the diurnal and the eternal. In theory, the latter encompasses the former, but neither can displace the other. Thus Daniel writes, in "To Honor One of the Poets":

To honor the God of this life
I try to see every configuration of
atom that constitutes the active
shutter speed of this
stuttering existence . . .
. . . .
God's elegant benevolence
under the circumstances.

The poet reaches for a synoptic vision of creation that embraces the greatest and least of its details, wryly suggesting that even divine will is conditioned in a phenomenal universe. To achieve such a perspective would, notionally, put the poet on an equal cognitive footing with the Deity, if not one of power. At the same time, though, the poet is equally obliged to move through the daily tasks that are his creaturely role:

To honor this life I get up and move in it,
scratch its cats, drink its water, drive its
roads, work for its pay checks.

Humility—the poet's proper stance—is restored by performing one's duties and accepting one's social no less than one's existential lot. Again, in "I'd Like a Pen," Daniel tries to imagine a simultaneity of vision that would capture a world beyond language, and with it a sense of how the world "adheres in true humility" to the divine plan in all its particulars. But such a language doesn't exist, and neither, he suspects, does such a world: he himself is sufficient proof of its imperfections. To give an adequate account of even a single detail of it is, moreover, beyond his capacity; as a summer heat wave ends, he writes: "The heat is broken by the patter of rain. I wish I could somehow get that / sound right . . ." ("The Heat Is Broken"). There is—the poet ceaselessly affirms—an underlying unity in all things, but never to be grasped except in difference: "Heavens //at a clang, high bells of song in silver clouds / our alarm clock at our / side" ("To Get to Sleep").

What we place faith in finally, Daniel suggests, is balance, that the sum of things is positive, however calamitous the particulars may appear in the moment. This, too, is a way of affirming an ultimate providence, for, he says, "the list of God's graces is endless, and goes on / longer than any litany of disasters, but maybe / more hidden . . ." ("A Cup of Crystal Water"). The 'hiddenness' of God lies partly in the distractions of a phenomenal world, and partly in the disparity between finite minds and the infinite one. Nonetheless, the "great arch" that symbolizes the hidden ends and burdened path of our temporal journey is also the rainbow of promise, and in the complex image that completes this poem

> at the
> beginning and end of each rainbow
> the Name of God [appears] in gold letters on a
> black field covered with
>
> white sheep sleepily chewing and showing us
> the true mercy in this
> idiosyncratic creation, and how
>
> perfect are God's strategies for
> getting to know Him.

The key image in Daniel's poetry is light: the Deity reveals himself as the light whose essence he is, the atom is a "sparkle" in air, and the poem is "a spot of light darting around on a / deep cavern wall" ("Some Say the Poem"). As this latter image suggests, darkness is—at least in our phenomenal world—the indispensable backdrop on which light appears, although what we get of it, often enough, is "Just a glimpse. Then / darkness again." But, as Daniel concludes this poem, "For a Moment I Glimpsed," this too is "God's good // pleasure undeceived."

All things in their many forms, Daniel suggests, offer the prayer of their being to the divine essence, including "light" itself ("Prayers of the Various"). Man, too, recalcitrant as he may be, cannot avoid his own prayer, which is that of the poem. Its job is to explore the given of this world, but its request is for what must finally elude it: "Lord, illumine the whole house // at last" ("'I'm Frightened of the Edge of the Abyss'").

Even in this volume, written almost two decades before his death, Daniel feels the approach of mortality. But it comes, too, with the assurance—or the further prayer?—that final revelation will come:

The door to God's door flings open.
"Enter now," we're commanded.

We slip out of this world like a coat
that falls to the floor behind us.

"Welcome," the Voice says with sweet
patience and peace.

"You're here."
("Door to the Presence")

I hope that's just where Daniel is right now.

BARDS ON FILM

by David Livewell

I am a night owl and was addicted to *The Charlie Rose Show* on PBS, which airs at midnight in the Philadelphia area. The two conditions went hand-in-hand for years. I need more sleep now, and I have a DVR to record the interview show. Sleep problem solved. I witnessed great, commercial-free conversations. I wished Charlie had more poets as guests. I was lucky enough to catch Seamus Heaney, Derek Walcott, Kay Ryan, and Stanley Kunitz on his program over the years. The intimacy of their voices drew me in. I felt closer to their gifts after seeing them in these intense conversations at the round, oak table against the black background. Those interviews primed me for longer documentaries about poets. In an age of visibility and saturation, how deeply should we know our poets? The frenzy for more biographical facts about Shakespeare or Dickinson never loses steam, and the lives often do shed more light on the dark mysteries of the poetry. I just saw a show about the contents of Shakespeare's grave. In 1995 the literary world was salivating when a previously unknown daguerreotype of Dickinson was discovered at a junk sale, as if even one more image of her could unlock a different aspect of her genius. Some very good novelists have taken up fictional accounts about conjectured incidents in the lives of Keats, Blake, Shakespeare, Poe, Dickinson, and others. There are levels of biography and obscurity.

My poetry-reading friends sometimes are reluctant to watch documentary films about poets. Maybe overly dramatic and inept biopics have soured them. Biographical dramas about artists, musicians, and writers can be disappointing. I'm reluctant to watch the new films about Hemingway or Miles Davis, for instance. Do we know any more about the poetry of Plath, Eliot, or Keats after seeing such fictionalized films as

Sylvia, or *Tom and Viv,* or *Bright Star?* Hollywood plays up
the tortured artists' painful lives and sheds little or no light
on the craft of writing. Although it would be boring to watch
a writer sitting all day at a desk, life and art are rarely separate
no matter how many literary theorists think otherwise. Poetry
emanates from the living body and through the mind. I go to
documentaries about my favorite poets to get more of them. I
watch to gain insight into the aspects of poets' lives that I
can't get from the page or from printed interviews. When a
great teaching poet dies, we often hear descriptions from
former students about how great the lectures were. Those
moments are lost forever for the rest of us.

Whenever I teach poetry in a university, I sense distrust for
the art form itself. The students trust their own feelings and
opinions in an age of social media, but they often distrust
poets (read Ben Lerner's recent treatise, *The Hatred of Poetry*).
They see poems as unnecessarily difficult, as puzzles that
can't be solved and are written for other poets. Films can
break down these misconceptions. Students can watch men
and women who have dedicated the best parts of themselves
to the art of poetry, the discipline of poetry with all its
pleasures and failures. That is the intensity that may be needed
to convince the next generation of readers that poetry is worth
pursuing. As a culture, we love difficult pursuits: sports,
singing, American Ninja Warrior, crossword puzzles, Sudoku,
and video games. Why would we want less of a challenge
from our literature?

Because poetry writing is a solitary act, it must be strange for
the poet when a film crew arrives at the door and the micro-
phones and cameras are set in place beside the bookshelves.
The poet must think, "What readers will care to watch this?"
Feature-length documentaries about contemporary poets are
a relatively recent phenomenon. These films exist as another
tool for readers. Poets' autobiographies can be filled with

exaggeration and may explain only certain dimensions of the poetry and life. Authorized and unauthorized biographies can confuse the matter even more. Does the biographer have an agenda (like the menacing Frost biography by Lawrance Thompson)? Did the poet's estate allow full access to diaries, letters, early drafts, etc.? Did friends and contemporaries co-operate or twist the truth to rewrite history? Such questions arose for me when reading biographies of Larkin, Frost, and Hughes. I wish all poets' biographies could be as informative, professional, and pleasurable as Langdon Hammer's recent biography of James Merrill. Likewise, I treasure the book-length interview that Dennis O'Driscoll conducted with Seamus Heaney (who died in 2013), but I almost dread any full-length, overly sincere biography that might be done about that Irish poet. A well-done documentary, however, can offer another path into a poet's work.

In addition to film documentaries, I enjoy podcasts and radio programs about poets. *The New Yorker*, The Poetry Foundation, RTE, and the BBC produce many of these quality programs. A reader also can watch online interviews with and readings by favorite poets like never before. But a filmed documentary takes us on a more layered journey. It gives us a visual dimension into the life and work. Poets are often more candid in casual conversation on film than they might be in their written responses, say to a *Paris Review* interviewer. We can get a sense of their domestic atmospheres, their speech patterns, their temperaments, their relatives, friends, their landscape and milieu—all factors that may have helped shape the poetry. We get a truer flavor of their personality, too. I began to search for films about poets to fill in some of the blanks. Because poetry and commerce do not go hand-in-hand, these films are not always in plain sight and often have meager marketing budgets.

A friend had me record some of my own poems for a few short films. He used still photography (mostly my own) that represented my subject matter. Many casual readers were drawn in with an excitement the printed page couldn't offer. The reactions were shocking to both of us. Viewers of the short films on YouTube sent the links to friends. We couldn't believe the number of hits they received—probably more than a year's worth of book sales. People were drawn more to the verse through the medium of the visual and the aural. Poetry is the oldest form of literature in most cultures, an oral tradition that is tied intrinsically to the memory and to the human voice. Perhaps new technologies return us to those ancient roots as if we sat again around the campfire listening to the local bard.

I hope *The American Masters* series will offer more poets. I am not enthralled with the poems of Carl Sandburg or Maya Angelou, but the films about those poets on PBS were well done, and their lives were often more interesting than the poems. *The American Masters* Walt Whitman feature channeled much more intensity than other programs in the series, and I also enjoyed their episode on the always-entertaining Allen Ginsberg (*The Life and Times of Allen Ginsberg*).

In general, the Beat poets are well represented on film. I watched another impressive, independent film on Ferlin-ghetti (*A Rebirth of Wonder*) and one that featured Gary Snyder and Jim Harrison conversing about the environment while taking a walk on the untouched trails of the central California coast (*The Practice of the Wild* from Whole Earth Films). It is refreshing to see films about serious living poets (although we just lost Mr. Harrison this year). Recently, I stumbled across a well-done film, *Robert Bly: A Thousand Years of Joy* (**www.robertblyfilm.com**). This poet crossed from the printed page into activism and social commentary.

Thinkers, actors, and writers (Jane Hirshfield, Gary Snyder, Philip Levine, and Donald Hall) describe this unique writer and talk about his cultural importance. He had friendships and ties to the Beats and the New York School of poets, but he made his own path and was outspoken about world peace and political matters. The film contains a lot of vintage footage as well: interviews, readings, demonstrations, and conferences.

I have yet to see the recent films about Alice Walker and Sonia Sanchez, but the trailers I found online were enticing. To celebrate National Poetry Month this year, several of these films were featured at The Poetry in Motion Film Festival (**http://rafaelfilm.cafilm.org/poetry-in-motion/**). More than one filmmaker told me that their only revenue came from individual DVD sales. With all the cable stations to choose from, it is sad that we can't have a government-funded station to support films about artists.

My earliest remembrance of films about poets was the PBS series, *Voices & Visions,* which aired in 1988. In 13 episodes, actors, critics, and poets explored some of the heavy hitters of American poetry: Crane, Whitman, Dickinson, Williams, Stevens, Hughes, Moore, Plath, Frost, Lowell, Bishop, Eliot, and Pound. Some of the talking heads included Richard Wilbur, Seamus Heaney, James Laughlin, Anthony Hecht, Helen Vendler, and Harold Bloom. Family members and friends were also interviewed. Although a bit dated now in their production value and pacing, these films remain histori-cally significant and can be viewed again for free on the Annen-berg Learner site (**http://www.learner.org/resources/series57.html**). Archival footage of the poets accompanies many of the poems.

Despite these American efforts, Ireland and Great Britain may have us beat by a long shot. Arts funding seems much more important across the pond. Many of my favorite poets are Irish or Scottish, so I was pleased to find great films about those poets. The BBC has offered consistent excellence in the field. I wish I could find them all in some central place. I have caught glimpses in BBC programs about Ted Hughes, Dylan Thomas, and John Betjeman. I would love to see all of the Omnibus episodes, especially a 1976 feature on one of my favorite Scottish poets, George Mackay Brown. In short clips I have seen, he walks the cobbled lanes of his beloved Stromness, a town in the Orkney Islands. We listen to him chat at his kitchen worktable and by the fire in his rocking chair. We feel the sensitivity, vulnerability, and charm that are present in his books. The National Library of Scotland has an impressive site where short films about poets are available (**http://movingimage.nls.uk/search.cfm?search_term=poet**). I urge a quick look there, especially at the program about the witty and talented Norman MacCaig who says, "[Poetry] GIVES YOU AN ENLARGED SENSITIVITY TO MINUTE THINGS WITH NO EXPENSE, EXCEPT PLEASURE." Also, two programs about the big gun, Hugh MacDiarmid, contain wonderful black-and-white footage of the poet. The Sorley MacClean piece is not to be missed either as he discusses his career. Scottish TV also offered a delightful little one-on-one interview show called *Off the Page*. On YouTube you can find episodes with the Scottish poets MacCaig, Alistair Reid, MacLean, Iain Crichton Smith, Liz Lochhead, and Edwin Morgan.

BBC Four produced an impressive-looking series with the poet-host Owen Sheers, *A Poet's Guide to Great Britain*. (The DVD collection came out in 2010.) Sheers is comfortable and compelling in front of the camera. He takes us to six locations, the settings of six famous British poems. We hear the poem while witnessing the stunning cinematography of their settings. We learn the background and the historical and artistic significance of each work. These short segments would be a great addition to any literature class.

I remember, in 1991, an excellent BBC South Bank program about Seamus Heaney. (I still cannot locate the South Bank Shows about Hughes, Larkin, and Betjeman.) The host, Melvyn Bragg (also a novelist), did a fantastic job interviewing Heaney about his new book, *Seeing Things*, while also taking the viewer on poetic journeys through the use of voice-overs and dramatized scenes from various poems. This was a great entrance into a new book. Heaney offered a bit of background to the poems in a way he might have done if one had the rare chance to sit down with him in a Dublin pub. He tells, for instance, why his 50th birthday led him to meditate on the smaller marvels in his life. The show made me buy the book immediately and read it with great anticipation.

I am haunted by a 1999 television (BBC and RTE) program (*Keeping Time*) that I was lucky enough to see through a friend. To celebrate his 60th birthday, filmmakers captured Heaney in a dilapidated country house reading his poetry. He stands at dramatic, rain-streaked windows to whisper his lines. He sits at rustic kitchen tables to recite childhood poems. He walks up grand staircases and strolls a ruined garden, reciting many of his most famous poems from memory. The scenes are bare and intense, as if you're witnessing private moments of poetic enlightenment in a time-ravaged space. Interspersed with the quiet readings, Liam O'Flynn, a good friend of Heaney's, appears in other echoing rooms playing traditional Irish music on the uilleann pipes and a tin whistle, a powerful combined effect. On Amazon, the CD of the readings and music is available, *The Poet & the Piper*. I recommend it highly.

I sought out more films. I obtained copies of *Out of the Marvellous* and *Personal Places,* both issued by RTE in Ireland. The former is a full-length documentary (out on DVD) about Heaney's poetry and career. The latter is a riveting documentary about an Irish poet who is lesser known in the United States, Thomas Kinsella.

We hear from Heaney's wife, his friends, and colleagues. We follow him to readings at Harvard, sit with him in his living room, accompany him on drives to his writing cottage in the country, and follow the trajectory of his road to the Nobel Prize. He and his wife sit on a couch and discuss the circumstances around the Nobel announcement in a candid interview. I look back now and realize how fortunate we are to have Heaney on film at 50, 60, and then 70 years of age. We follow his literary and personal progression.

Even though Kinsella spent most of his working years teaching at U.S. universities, his work is sometimes hard to find here. As a leading poet and a translator of early Irish poetry, Kinsella led the generation just before Heaney. He helped to found the Dolmen Press with Liam Miller at a time when few Irish presses existed to support poets. When that press met its demise, he created his own Peppercanister Press for pamphlet publication of his own poems. For many years he lived in Philadelphia while teaching at Temple University.

Films and recordings gain importance because we are losing senior poets at an astonishing rate. I am thankful that some were caught on film, but I wish some director had filmed features on Galway Kinnell, Mark Strand, Philip Levine, Theodore Roethke, Thom Gunn, James Merrill, Daniel Hoffman, Stanley Kunitz, Adrienne Rich, Amy Clampitt, Robert Lowell, and Jack Gilbert. I would add Elizabeth Bishop to this list, but there was a 2015 feature documentary about her houses and lovers. The film travels to Canada, Brazil, and the U.S. Although interesting, the film lacked Bishop's spirit. It felt stilted. Bishop continued to avoid labels and biographical facts, as she would have wished.

There is still world enough and time to catch Richard Wilbur, Wendell Berry (although there is a great Bill Moyers interview with Berry), Robert Pinsky, Mary Oliver, Linda Gregg, Charles Simic, and David Ferry on film. Samuel Menasche, chosen for a Neglected Masters Award from the Poetry Foundation before he died, can be found in two short films available on YouTube and Vimeo (*Life Is Immense* and *The Concise Poet*). Through her short and witty poems, it is clear that Kay Ryan must have admired this little-known poet. He didn't teach and wasn't published much in America. He lived a barebones existence in a New York, rent-controlled walk-up and had all of his poems memorized. The films offer domestic portraits of a private and dedicated writer. His exactitude and exuberance are contagious.

In Ireland right now I hope someone is filming Paul Muldoon, Michael Coady, Eiléan Ní Chuilleanáin, Peter Fallon, Medbh McGuckian , Paul Durcan, and Ciaran Carson. In Scotland, perhaps portraits could be filmed about Stewart Conn, Kathleen Jamie, or Douglas Dunn. In England, dispatch the video crews to Wendy Cope and Simon Armitage (alas, a bit too late for the recently deceased Geoffrey Hill). Through the years, I have corresponded with several filmmakers who say that poets, initially, are skeptical and reluctant about the prospect of a film. A larger release of quality material may change their minds.

A year before his early death (at 58) in 1999, Michael Hartnett, an emotional and troubled Irish poet, was the subject of a wonderful 40-minute film, *Michael Hartnett: A Necklace of Wrens* (Harvest Films). The documentary serves as a legacy to Hartnett's rich poems. For a time, he abandoned English and wrote only in Irish as a statement against English oppression. The film returns him to the places of his upbringing and the landscapes that shaped him. His recitations and reminiscences about his Irish-speaking grandmother are riveting. Heaney and others discuss his importance to Irish letters. After a brief writing life, we are thankful to have a bit more of him in his natural surroundings.

For another recent example on Vimeo, I found a 2012 documentary about the Irish poet and novelist, Dermot Healy (*The Writing in the Sky*). He died in 2014. This film stands out in my mind. It is very original and very artistic. We view his breathtaking seaside home in Sligo and watch with him as geese make their yearly and noisy flight above his house. This yearly ceremony comes to represent the sense of wonder in his late work. I didn't know this writer's verse previously, but the portrait was filmed so passionately that I was drawn in. Since watching I have sought out many of the works mentioned, and I'm still reading them with pleasure.

A short, but comprehensive 30-minute film about the Irish poet Desmond O'Grady (who also died in 2014) was made by Adam Wyeth and Keat Walsh, *A Life in a Day of Desmond O'Grady*. This important poet and translator was quite a character. We follow him through the locales of his beloved Kinsale. Through his poetry alone we would not have witnessed conversations about his famous acquaintances in various countries: Picasso, Beckett, Pound, Passolini, Bacon, Burroughs, and Fellini (and O'Grady's small role in *La Dolce Vita*).

From Loopline Films (**http://loopline.com/patrick-kavanagh-no-mans-fool/**), through the kind assistance of the director, Sé Murray Doyle, I watched a detailed and sympathetic documentary about the very survival of Patrick Kavanagh (*No Man's Fool*) in a country that gave him little notice during his lifetime. A former lover speaks on film for the first time and offers new insights about the tender nature of the private man.

Two Irish naturalists, Michael Viney and David Cabot, made a quiet and beautifully reverent documentary about Michael Longley's visits to Carrigskeewaun in County Mayo (*The Corner of the Eye*, Wild Goose Films, 1989). It was shown on RTE. Mr. Cabot graciously sent along a copy of the film and answered my questions. Michael Longley is a Belfast poet (and we do see him briefly in his Belfast home and neighborhood), but he fell in love with a vast, rugged, and lovely landscape in Mayo that kept him coming back year after year. He estimates that half of his poetry has been inspired by this place. He learned the names of the local birds and flowers and those details appear time and again in his poetry. Because this place is not his home or place of origin, he recognizes it as a place to encounter his deepest self and a place to pay attention to the smallest characteristics of this landscape. The place, in turn, has become his spiritual and poetic home.

Although I knew the work of the Irish poet, Derek Mahon, I was still intrigued by a 2010 film about him that a friend shared (*Derek Mahon: The Poetry Nonsense*). Filmed in four locales that Mahon called home, the documentary sheds light on a fairly reclusive author. I have seen Mahon read at a local college, but he does not court the limelight. This film gives a clearer view of his life and aesthetic, another reason to value such films. The reader can understand his sense of displacement, identity, and loss and approach the poems on the page with new insight. The intellect behind the poems is staggering. I had thought his verse was cold in some parts, but this film returned me to his work afresh. Now I hear the voice of a complex man and poet. Biographical criticism alone would not allow these visceral revelations.

So America has some catching up to do. How many important poets have died who would have made fine subjects for short films? As a young writer and before the expansion of the internet, I ordered several VHS tapes from The Lannan

Foundation, including interviews with and readings by Philip Levine, Jack Gilbert, Richard Wilbur, and Hayden Carruth. These may be the only filmed glimpses we have of some of these poets. Many are online now. And in 2009 the American Academy of Poets did a wonderful DVD, *The Poet's View*, profiling John Ashbery, Louise Glück, Anthony Hecht, Kay Ryan, C.K. Williams, and W.S. Merwin. The viewer can watch the poets in their homes while they casually discuss their art in short but informative segments. I hope there are plans for more.

Recently, however, I stumbled upon two films now out on DVD. Both are exceptional. The first is a film produced by Ida Does about the Saint Lucian poet, Derek Walcott (**http://www.walcottfilm.com/**). Walcott won the Nobel Prize in 1992 (three years before his friend, Seamus Heaney, who also appears in the film). He is now 86. He may be slower when he walks, but his speech and memory are sharp. *Poetry Is an Island* derives its title from a line in his Nobel Prize acceptance speech: "Poetry is an island that breaks away from the main." Poetry and islands can seem marginal to casual observers, but they are worlds unto themselves. We watch his development as a writer, from poor island beginnings to the world stage. We tour that dilapidated childhood home and imagine the presence of the young Walcott in every room. A wonderful story stands out about how his mother paid for his first book of poems. What a miracle that she gathered the money at all. He never looked back. He had to write.

We learn how the very rhythm of the sea and island life helped create his temperament and the rhythmic components of his sophisticated and memorable verse. Creation and island life are his private joys. Walcott is blunt and often emotional in the interviews. He is an old man compelled to speak the truth while he still has time. He offers memorable recollections about his childhood, deceased friends, colonialism, and an ever-changing ecology on the island. The natural beauty of the Saint Lucia that Walcott remembers is now threatened by resort developers. We see how he uses his celebrity to voice his opinions about these dangers. He doesn't want the past forgotten or the landscape that shaped his mind destroyed. We are brought into the vivid tropical world of the island and get a complete portrait of the still-working artist.

In fact, Walcott is a formidable painter and playwright as well. We see him in his studio. We watch his interactions with local actors during a play rehearsal. We attend a party at his house and can be a fly on the wall when Seamus Heaney flies in for an emotional (and, it turns out, final) visit. One of the most moving participants is Walcott's childhood friend, who also passed away just after the filming. Walcott's wife and son supply striking commentary as well.

The island scenes are far from the footage we see of his Nobel Prize acceptance speech. The contrast in his personal history makes these moments more memorable. Moving from Boston to Stockholm, and then back again to his roots, the film will turn viewers back to the poetry, plays, and paintings. Since the filming, Walcott's childhood home has been chosen for a full restoration by the government. It is clear that the screening must have encouraged local authorities to rescue that dwelling from oblivion. The educational role of these films cannot be stressed enough. Poetry can make something happen when it reaches people who are ready for its gifts. It is certain that poetry changed the lives of poets.

For a more recent example, we can turn to W.S. Merwin. In April 2016, to commemorate National Poetry Month, many PBS stations aired a documentary about Merwin, now 89 and going blind, a former Poet Laureate, two-time Pulitzer winner, and an unmatched environmentalist who lives in Maui. The original film which is a bit longer, is called *W.S. Merwin:*

Even Though the Whole World is Burning (**http://www.eventhoughthewholeworldisburning.com/**). The TV version has been shortened and renamed: *W.S. Merwin: To Plant a Tree.*

The film's original title is excerpted from a Merwin poem called "Rain Light" about a powerful memory/vision of the poet's mother. The PBS title is from a couplet in his poem "Place": "On the last day of the world / I would want to plant a tree." In the journey of the film, we learn how the lines of both poems inform his vision as a writer, Buddhist, and conservationist. The natural world proved a comfort to him, even during his upbringing in the industrial landscape of New Jersey. He asked about a weed growing up between the cracks of the sidewalk, and his mother informed him that the whole earth lurked under the concrete. That moment proved unforgettable in the forming of his imagination. It is fitting that in old age the poet would restore the seemingly useless 19 acres around his Hawaiian home in Maui and plant and foster one of the largest private palm forests in the world.

Merwin's wife, Paula Schwartz, offers a description of his daily working life: how he rises in the morning and sits on their balcony overlooking the palms. He drinks tea while reading and scribbling. She never sees a poem until it is finished and placed on the table. Daily attention to craft remains vital. The rest of the day is consumed with the planting and pruning of the palm trees.

J.D. McClatchy, poet and editor of *The Yale Review*, and Harold Bloom, esteemed critic and scholar, offer wonderful commentary about Merwin and his literary achievements. Bloom even sheds some tears over the utter beauty of Merwin's unadorned lines, lines that have abandoned almost all punctuation. The bare essentials of speech matter the most to Merwin.

The film describes his upbringing under a stern minister father. Hymns were the first poetry that engaged him. He studied under John Berryman and took advice from Ezra Pound about translating poems from as many languages as possible. He lived in a rural French village for a time to experience fully the cycles of the seasons. Eventually, studying with a Zen Buddhist master brought him to Maui. He decided to stay, mesmerized by the beauty of the land and the folklore of the people. A Merwin Conservancy will preserve his beloved palms long after he is gone. This film's scope and pacing are entrancing. We feel like Merwin's invited visitor in a magical landscape created from nothing. Merwin reminds us that we live in our memories. The present is passing us by every moment.

Although I found many films through online searches, I must thank the filmmakers and companies who provided me with DVDs. Ida Does kindly answered my questions and sent me her exquisite Walcott film. Stefan Schaefer kindly sent along his wide-reaching Merwin film right after it appeared in film festivals. David Cabot from County Mayo was kind enough to offer a copy of his film about Michael Longley. Haydn Reiss supplied me with a copy of his Robert Bly film, a film based on the journals of William Stafford called Every War Has Two Losers (with commentary by Bly, Merwin, Alice Walker, and others. Reiss sent a third film about the literary friendship between Bly and William Stafford. The two friends read in front of a small audience and walk together in the woods talking about family, nature, pacifism, and writing. Stafford reminds us that poems are gifts, small miracles that arrive out of nowhere and then demand revision and critical attention. Chris Felver was kind enough to send me his Ferlinghetti film.

In a way these films resemble travel documentaries. We visit actual localities and explore the landscapes of the poets' imaginations. I don't suggest that these films are fuller experiences than a reader sitting with a silent poem on a page. That encounter should come first. Think, however, of the young in classrooms. Today's students are visually oriented, and films may be the engaging tool that can allow them to enter the rich world of poetry for the first time. Live theatre or film often help students engage with Shakespeare for the first time, giving them a way into the language. The Poetry Archive in London (**http://www.poetryarchive.org/**), an online site of audio clips of poets reading their own works, can bring poetry alive to students as well. I have used readings from this site in my university classrooms with great success, and I didn't have to lug in a stack of CDs.

I have learned a lot from watching poets in these filmed moments. They remind me how powerful and singular a poetic vision can be. These poets wrote to rescue and transform their memories and their local landscapes. We see firsthand what they loved, their private worlds. I kept thinking of Keats' term, "the holiness of the heart's affections," and how imagination and language distinguish us from other animals because of our affections. These poets tried to preserve an authentic life filled with artistic discovery. When poetry transforms a reader, it has already transformed the lives of the men and women who made it. It is fitting that the word "muse" derives from the Latin where it connotes carrying something in uncertainty and silence. Sacrifice and fidelity to their art helped these poets carry their gifts through uncertainty and silence. I feel I witnessed some of those journeys. Desmond O'Grady, in his feature, summed it up this way: "Live full lives. Leave some record."

Poets and film, like poets and radio, can create a loving marriage, fulfilling our appetite for heightened language, fresh perspectives, and new environments. Maybe more of these films will make it to television and cable in the future. I hope that the Poetry Foundation or The Lannan Foundation might support some of these efforts, so that poetry fans do not have to search this hard to find such captivating films.

POLITICS AND THE ENGLISH-LANGUAGE HAIKU:
LEARNING FROM GEORGE ORWELL

by Michael Dylan Welch

In 1946 George Orwell wrote "Politics and the English Language," an essay that is still quoted by writing teachers today. Without too much effort, we can also apply what it has to say to haiku, both the writing of these little gems and to criticism about them as well.

I've just referred to haiku as little gems. This is a deliberate ploy. Such a phrase is an example of what Orwell decries. We say these poems are "precious" because we have received that language from others. But it has become stale. Marlene Mountain says that "haiku is not a port in a storm." Haiku is not a cute and precious gem, and as long as we view it that way, we are stuck not just in stale language but stale thought, and the haiku we write will not rise into literature. Orwell wants us to find fresh thoughts about what we are saying and, if necessary, fresh metaphors. That doesn't mean we have to make everything new, but to think freshly—or, as Jane Hirshfield has put it, to "make it yours."

Orwell begins his essay by presenting five convoluted passages of text where thought has been suffocated by needlessly complex and obscure language. He explores how the imagery is stale and how grasping at complexity leads to a lack of precision. He unpacks the tricks their authors use to dodge responsible writing, which amount to using dying metaphors, verbal false limbs, pretentious diction, and meaningless words, all of which he explains. I won't quote the passages here, or Orwell's commentary on them, not just because you can read the essay for yourself, but because my point lies beyond their reefs. Along the way, Orwell says something I've said in haiku workshops for years, that "Bad writers . . . are nearly always haunted by the notion that Latin or Greek words are grander than Saxon ones," and explains how certain words in art and literary criticism have become meaningless. By this and other means, our little gems are simply dull.

I will, however, quote a passage from *Ecclesiastes* that Orwell translates to illustrate the obfuscation that can too easily occur in writing—and I would say in haiku and other poetry criticism:

> I returned and saw under the sun, that the race is not to the swift, nor the battle to the strong, neither yet bread to the wise, nor yet riches to men of understanding, nor yet favour to men of skill; but time and chance happeneth to them all.

Here is Orwell's partial translation:

> Objective considerations of contemporary phenomena compel the conclusion that success or failure in competitive activities exhibits no tendency to be commensurate with innate capacity, but that a considerable element of the unpredictable must invariably be taken into account.

He says that "Every such phrase anaesthetizes a portion of one's brain." Here's what else he has to say on these passages—observations that students of haiku will be able to apply to their poetry:

> The first contains forty-nine words but only sixty syllables, and all its words are those of everyday life. The second contains thirty-eight words of ninety syllables: eighteen of those words are from Latin roots, and one from Greek. The first sentence contains six vivid images, and only one phrase ("time and chance") that could be called

vague. The second contains not a single fresh, arresting phrase, and in spite of its ninety syllables it gives only a shortened version of the meaning contained in the first. Yet without a doubt it is the second kind of sentence that is gaining ground in modern English.

Orwell points out, with the second passage, how easily language can become pretentious and meaningless because we too easily repeat what we have heard before ("objective considerations" and the like). This is possible not just in commentary about haiku but in haiku themselves, where we too often write what everyone else has written (part of what I call "déjà-ku"). But in criticism, the larger danger is pretentiousness and meaninglessness, and academic posturing that leads to alienation. He says that "it is natural to fall into a pretentious, Latinized style" and that, "By using stale metaphors, similes, and idioms, you save much mental effort, at the cost of leaving your meaning vague, not only for your reader but for yourself." Orwell sums himself up:

As I have tried to show, modern writing at its worst does not consist in picking out words for the sake of their meaning and inventing images in order to make the meaning clearer. It consists in gumming together long strips of words which have already been set in order by someone else, and making the results presentable by sheer humbug. The attraction of this way of writing is that it is easy. It is easier—even quicker, once you have the habit—to say *In my opinion it is not an unjustifiable assumption that* than to say *I think.*

Orwell offers these solutions, and they apply to haiku poetry as much as to haiku criticism:

> A scrupulous writer, in every sentence that he writes, will ask himself at least four questions, thus: What am I trying to say? What words will express it? What image or idiom will make it clearer? Is this image fresh enough to have an effect? And he will probably ask himself two more: Could I put it more shortly? Have I said anything that is avoidably ugly? But you are not obliged to go to all this trouble. You can shirk it by simply throwing your mind open and letting the ready-made phrases come crowding in.

Let me swim into the lagoon, and talk more about haiku rather than haiku criticism. Perhaps the most quoted single phrase of Orwell's essay is that "The great enemy of clear language is insincerity." We can get to good haiku by being sincere. It's really that simple, and it helps if we balance that with knowledge of the literature and its techniques while guarding against repeating the old and tiresome phrasings of others. For me, too, haiku arise out of empathy, of putting ourselves where the other person or other thing is—to learn of the pine from the pine, as Bashō told us. We have to pay attention. As American psychologist and Buddhist meditation expert Tara Brach has said, "Attention is the most basic form of love." And haiku arise out vulnerability, too, where our poems make us vulnerable by saying "this matters to me." They also pull on the vulnerability of others, if our poem makes a connection when a reader agrees that "this matters to me too." Sparrows with huddled necks, an elevator opening and closing. It all boils down to sincerity, and we can get there through empathy, attention, and vulnerability. Do we mean what we say, or are we just repeating what others have said?

Here is a rundown of other advice Orwell provides, which haiku poets can apply to their work:

1. Scrap "every word or idiom which has outworn its usefulness."
2. Use "the fewest and shortest words that will cover one's meaning."
3. Above all, "let the meaning choose the word, and not the other way around."

"In prose," Orwell adds (and with poetry too), "the worst thing one can do with words is surrender to them. When you think of a concrete object, you think wordlessly, and then, if you want to describe the thing you have been visualising you probably hunt about until you find the exact words that seem to fit it." Could that be any more strongly applicable to haiku? Haiku begin with images, and our personal experiences of everything we see, hear, smell, touch, and taste. We have feelings as a result, and by trusting the image we can impart those same feelings to the reader (Eliot's "objective correlative" comes into play with haiku). It all starts with an image that is concrete—and wordless. I believe it was R. H. Blyth who first referred to haiku as a "wordless" poem, a notion picked up by D. T. Suzuki and Alan Watts, and then explored in detail by Eric Amann in his 1969 book *The Wordless Poem*. In Volume 1 of *Haiku*, from 1949, Blyth has a section on wordlessness, which he describes as one of thirteen "characteristics of the state of mind which the creation and appreciation of haiku demand" (154). He says that haiku is "essentially a *wordless* state, in which words are used, not to express anything, but rather to clear away something that seems to stand between us and the real things which . . . are then perceived by self-knowledge" (176). Orwell also reminds us of that wordless origin of what we are trying to say, and asks us to use the simplest words to present that wordlessness, and the intuitions we have as a result. As he puts it, "Probably it is better to put off using words as long as possible and get one's meaning as clear as one can through pictures and sensations. Afterward one can choose—not simply *accept*—the phrases that will best cover the meaning, and then switch round and decide what impressions one's words are likely to make on another person."

I like how Orwell asserts the act of choosing rather than merely accepting the words needed to convey our meaning—to describe that falling maple leaf or the cracking of an heirloom bowl. We need to be conscientious and involved. It can be lazy to assume that the first thought is always the best thought. Ginsberg revised the hell out of things. More importantly, I also like how Orwell ends with a nod to the audience, since the aim of haiku is to communicate with readers (the purpose of haiku, as William J. Higginson has told us, is to share them). "One can often be in doubt about the effect of a word or a phrase," Orwell says, "and one needs rules that one can rely on when instinct fails." He then offers the following six rules that apply to haiku just as much as they do to any other kind of writing:

1. Never use a metaphor, simile, or other figure of speech which you are used to seeing in print.
2. Never use a long word where a short one will do.
3. If it is possible to cut a word out, always cut it out.
4. Never use the passive where you can use the active.
5. Never use a foreign phrase, a scientific word, or a jargon word if you can think of an everyday English equivalent.
6. Break any of these rules sooner than say anything outright barbarous.

Orwell concludes that "These rules sound elementary, and so they are, but they demand a deep change of attitude in anyone who has grown used to writing in the style now fashionable." He was talking of the 1940s, but styles of writing fashionable today are equally problematic. To return to the Bible, in *Matthew* and *Mark* it says that the poor will always be with us, and so it seems to be with haiku. But by coming back to the advice that Orwell offers, perhaps there is a stay against poorness of language that can enrich all our haiku— and polish some of our precious little gems into diamonds.

Orwell's essay is online in several places. Here's one of them: http://www.orwell.ru/library/essays/politics/english/e_polit

ENCOUNTERING CIORAN

by Daniel Lawless

As with so many things – films, cities, bourbon – there are writers one comes to too early or too late. In the latter category, I would include, oh, Salinger, Mailer, Saint-Exupéry, the usual suspects; in the former, Sartre, Bernhard, Coetzee – and Cioran.

A chronic truant and general miscreant in my adolescence, nevertheless I was a *reader* – if an undisciplined one. Long afternoons at the Louisville Public Library, which seemed to me then at once forbidding and enchanted – a great grey castle-like building with tall windows of cylinder glass. Sometimes I'd come with a recommendation in hand – one author alludes to another, or a name pops up in an index. Mostly, however, I'd leave it to chance: head to Literature, or Poetry, or Philosophy, and find whatever I'd find. So it was I arrived at Cioran's doorstep, at age seventeen. I remember the encounter almost perfectly. For some reason, I'd paused at the "French" section – not that I could read a word of the language; no doubt I recognized a few names I'd perused in translation: Artaud (*The Theater and Its Double*), Cendrars, half a dozen of the Surrealists. Then, *Précis de decomposition*. To an alienated (!), cynical, self-absorbed (is there another type?) teenager of a literary cast, the title alone, with its air of ghoulish academe: catnip. Nor was I at all disappointed when I flipped through the pages, finding now under the heading *Certains Matins,*

"*Regret de n'étre pas Atlas, de ne pouvoir secourer les épaules pour assister à l'écroulement de cette risible matière…*" [1]

(Yes! Hadn't I too, longed to shake off this stupid world? That sentence alone took me ten minutes to decode, with a French-English Dictionary.)

Now, "*Quand on ne peut se deliverer de soi, on se délecte à se dévorer.*" [2] (I had already been diagnosed with an ulcer; it would burst and nearly cost me my life in a few years.)

Picking up another book, *Syllogismes de l'amertume*, there was this felicitous observation:

"*L'odeur de la créature nous met sur la piste d'une divinité fétide.*" – a *foul* God, as foul (and omnipotent) as I knew myself to be! [3]

And so on.

Disappointed? How could I have been? Listen to Kimball's 1991 dismissal of Cioran in *The New Criterion*: "…a *style* [italics mine] that blends an almost Olympian coolness and intellectuality with the appearance of passion bordering, at times, on hysteria…essentially an adolescent style: high-handed, confessional, histrionic, but nevertheless full of energy."

---

[1] The regret of not being Atlas, of not being able to shrug my shoulders and watch all this silly matter collapse.

[2] When one cannot free oneself from oneself, one delights in devouring oneself.

[3] The creature's scent puts us on the track of a fetid divinity.

Well, yeah.

So, in one sense *not* too early: for even if that "reappraisal" were altogether true, didn't Cioran give me exactly what I needed, then? What Kerouac, Ginsberg, Warhol, Johnny Rotten have always given to their fans – a vision or version-presentation of their own *Weltanschauung* – though they might not know they had one? A glimpse of what their own stylistic preferences might comprise; mirror in which they might find *themselves* reflected for once, perfected, their inchoate rage and limpid yearnings legitimized, even encouraged?

But it isn't, is it? True, I mean, Kimball's assessment. At least not altogether. Isn't it also possible Sontag was right, that Cioran's

"...kind of writing is meant for readers who in a sense already know what he says; they have traversed these vertiginous thoughts for themselves. Cioran doesn't make any of the usual efforts to "persuade," with his oddly lyrical chains of ideas, his merciless irony, his gracefully delivered allusions to nothing less than the whole of European thought since the Greeks. An argument is to be "recognized," and without too much help. Good taste demands that the thinker furnish only pithy glimpses of intellectual and spiritual torment. Hence, Cioran's tone—one of immense dignity, dogged, sometimes playful, often haughty. But despite all that may appear as arrogance, there is nothing complacent in Cioran, unless it be his very sense of futility and his uncompromisingly elitist attitude toward the life of the mind"?

And if she *is* correct, and I think she is, then, in a more profound way, I was indeed too early – far, far too early, as I have learned over the half-century since. I simply had not read enough to capture a tenth of Cioran's allusions, let alone decipher his relentless, playful paradoxes. To say nothing of appreciating his exquisite, yes, style.

So, split the difference – too early, but also right on time.

For the moment, let's return to that long-ago boy, that long-ago library. Four books in all, including *La Tentation d'exister*, and *De l'inconvénient d'être né*. I must have remained entranced there for a good eight hours, on the floor with its ancient stained scarlet carpet (coffee, and were those cigarette burns?) until closing time, shifting my attentions from one book to another dictionary in hand, when I noticed it had grown dark. Gathering my bounty, I paused to peek at the little sign-out sheet under each cover, wondering what kindred spirit might have walked these same purgatorial alleyways before me. Virginal. Not one had been checked out. I knew what I had to do.

In those days, of course, there were no detectors stationed at the massive oak doors that faced the check-out desk to alert absent-minded patrons of their clerical requirements – or nab would-be thieves. So: out I went, my army coat pockets rather heavier than when I had entered.

(Would he have approved? I was certain of it. Just as, a few months previous, I had taken Merton for a rebel; before that Husymans a traitor.)

At home that evening, and for many evenings to follow, I could be found (by whom? a figure of speech; I was an isolate *by decree*, as C. says somewhere), poring over the work, line by line, word by word, with that trusty paperback Webster's. Cioran became the first writer whose entire *oeuvre* I read – those in French as well as Richard Howard's marvelous English translations. Nor has my enthusiasm, tempered by age as it might be, waned in any substantial way. (I have read and read him again, and again, as some their Bible or their Pynchon. A 62 year old fan boy.)

Tonight, as I write these few words, his face – that Bernstein-ian countenance with its unforgeable signature of suffering and intellect – is propped against the wall behind my desk. An insect, almost imperceptible, a moving *virgule,* traverses his cheek – without thinking I reach out to extinguish its life as one would a match-flame. Instantly, regret. Not for it but for *me. L'acte* Cioran-esque, let's call it.

READING (AND REREADING) CIORAN:
PRETERNATURAL SLACKER

by Daniel Lawless

A sentence I read somewhere whose paraprosdokian charm is undeniable: Beckett broke off his friendship with Cioran because he found him "too pessimistic."

At first glance, a pronouncement one takes to be a matter of degree: X has advanced beyond acceptable measures along an identified spectrum: Abramovic or, say, "The Aristocrats" – apotheosis of the dirty joke. A taking-too-far, in other words. But I don't think that's what Beckett meant, what caused the breakup, if only apocryphally. No, I think that can be put down to duration – Cioran was too *often* pessimistic. Like the hermits and mystics with whom he was fascinated and among which I think he himself should be situated (to his credit and horror no doubt), Cioran is *insupportable* by reason of a maddening single-mindedness. Not a quality (narcissistic, tiresome) many friendships are built to endure, however much we might want it to be otherwise.

("Charm," too, a descriptor I choose not unadvisedly: from the Latin, carmen: song, verse, *incantation* -- repetitious wordiness used to conceal a lack of content. Indictments (except wordiness, of course) often leveled at Cioran and, at one time or another, at such disparate figures as the authors of Genesis and The Illiad, Cervantes, Pound, Durrell, Woolfe, Marcuse, Knausgaard. That last of particular interest, by the way, and to whom I'll return in a moment, to conclude this brief rumination on the effects of a lifetime's reading of Cioran.

First, though, a day-trip to the usual why-I-read so-and-so tourist traps:

He is sui generis. Close your eyes, stick your finger in any book by Cioran, and ask yourself, Could anyone else have written this passage? E.g.,

Every neophyte being a spoilsport, once someone gets excited over anything, even my own vagaries, I prepare for a rift – and my revenge.

Or,

What is a "contemporary"? Someone you'd like to kill, without quite knowing how.

Or,

The mediocrity of my grief at funerals. Impossible to feel sorry for the deceased; conversely, every birth casts me into consternation. It is incomprehensible, it is insane that people can show a baby, that they can exhibit this potential disaster and rejoice over it.

The case has been made for crowning Cioran "The Last Philosopher in Europe"; as these passages indicate (and there are literally hundreds like them) a better or at least equally valid title might be "The Last *Comedian* in Europe." Sui generis, yes, and wildly funny – a quality I have savored perhaps more than any other over the years.

Party of One. Close on the above is the fact of his obdurate obscurity, which nevertheless I have found comforting: the evergreen frisson of the undiscovered bistro or *boite.* Relief that there is no school or movement tagged Cioran-ian, too. Try as you will to file him under "misanthrope" or "nihilist" or some such drivel (though you might consider "insomniaacs"), in the sense that there are Lacanians, or Tillich-ians he has resisted for some seventy-odd years academic pigeonholing and largely evaded the depredations of the dissertation, an oversight of fantastic stupidity for which we all can be grateful. (Or perhaps not an oversight but integral to the nature of the aphoristic style. As Cioran observes, professors can't do anything with it, can't annotate or categorize its position: "When they read a book of aphorisms, they say, 'Oh, look what this fellow said ten pages back, now he's saying the contrary. He's not serious.'")

No better testimony on this subject than Charles Simic's, who asks in his *New York Review of Books* piece from 2010,

Who reads E.M. Cioran nowadays? Someone must, since most of his books have been translated and are in print. At universities where graduate students and professors are familiar with every recent French philosopher and literary theorist, he's practically unknown, though he was a much finer thinker and wrote far better prose than a whole lot of them.

Tribal Marker. Just as in sixties' (or before) western gay semiotics the left-or right-side positioned handkerchief, earing, or keychain signified sexual preferences, or as the above-mentioned "The Aristocrats" has served as a kind of secret handshake for in-the-know comedians at least since vaude-ville days, I have found dropping the name "Cioran" in casual conversation (unlikely as that might sound), or in a letter or email, to be a reliable assessor of my correspondent's literary (even psycho-social) predilections. A blank stare or its written equivalent is, per Simic, all too often the response and suggests our acquaintance for as long as it lasts will be fundamentally flawed, at odds and ends. On the other hand, an enthusiastic response – I've never received any other kind from those who've actually read him – means approximately some variation of: Ah, comrade! Cioran as the *PiL* button of ye olde punk days.

The Pleasures of the Aphorism. I know, Cioran is an essayist, though I don't think this is his natural métier. Nor is it why I am here, nor likely why you have read or will read Cioran one day: that would be because you stumbled across one of his aphorisms. Like the poet Don Paterson writing in

The Telegraph in 2004, these years I, too, "pass much of my time in a state of guilt-ridden paralysis, [from which] I emerge most days with nothing to show for my efforts but 40 e-mails, a dead leg and an empty box of Solpadeine (substitute reserved supplies of Tylenol # 3)." Which is to say that I, like Paterson, value the notion of, after all that too-often pointless and diversionary reading, "rescuing something from the day." How welcome, then, the aphorism -- its brevity and lightning-strike nature so arresting to the benumbed mind. And Paterson gives it its mordant due: "...no one ever sewed Thackeray into the lining of their greatcoat as they marched off to the trenches. It was Marcus Aurelius or Pascal." But where Mr. Paterson sees only "rubbish" in the second advertisement for the aphorism, its tone, we part ways. For him, that tone is enormously irritating: "...one of absolute self-certainty. The aphorism talks to you as if you were an idiot. This also makes them all sound rather generic, like the ravings of some wee disenfranchised god, bellowing away in the abyss to no one in particular." Close to home, yes, and I feel the brush of that assertion's ragged fingernails sometimes. But, usually I find in this certainty precisely what I crave. Why? Maybe because as an editor and poet I read a lot of poetry, whose insights or apercus -- aphorisms of a sort -- are almost always fatally collegial, wan, qualified and re-qualified, delivered almost as questions, *aslant,* as the famous adjective has it. They intimate – with a flourish: a certain flattery of the reader or sheepishness often lingers about them, as if to mumble, "Of course, you, gentle reader, know this... "Also, a self-conscious, off-putting timidity, an odor of the humble-brag: "I'm not sure, what do you think, is it possible that...? " One tires of feigned humility, of courtesy, at last, suffused as it is with a displaced servility. Like Cubs fans and certain fetishists, one longs to be treated abysmally sometimes, taken for an idiot: even the monologue of a twee deity, barked into the void, can be preferable to the acceptable, well-appointed whisper of a talented *friend*. (Which in another universe and another context might explain the mystery of Trump – god forbid.) Not to mention, the "aphorisms" of poetry all too rarely reside anywhere but the work's final lines; the reader is more or less sumptuously frogmarched through the author's let's-pretend-this-isn't-all-set-up in order to get to the "wise-saying." Surely there are exceptions, many, but a frequent enough occurrence as to discompose.

Which brings us to the matter of Cioran's **style,** whose elegance and lucidity moved St.-John Perse to proclaim him "one of the greatest French writers to honor our language since the death of Paul Valery." What did Sontag say? "That most *delicate* of minds..." Outside of Barthes, perhaps, who else in philosophy is so imbued with a sense of the fine-ness of words, their wonders and conceits? (Cioran loved Dickinson, by the way – how right that seems.) Again, the work of others – Valery, yes, and Char, Davidowitz, Cocteau, Krause, Bierce, Lichtenberg, Jabbes, Chesterton, Santayana, La Bruyere, et.al. – would seem to contradict this point. But look again: which of these sustains our interest over the long haul, fascinates and challenges us with such astonishing regularity? Maybe we take Cioran's accomplishments for granted – see: Jordan, Picasso, Pei. You will say it is in the quality of his thought that his genius lies, and I would assent, but add: read the words. They are the distillation of ideas, as poems are, yet Cioran has distilled even the poem to its essence (the image), rather like the Surrealists, whom he detested, I imagine, who had no use for narratives or context. To the question posed by some interviewer as to why he chose to write in this manner, he replied laconically, and one assumes perfectly disingenuously given his prodigious output:
I'm not sure exactly. I think it was a phenomenon of laziness perhaps... Aphorisms are conclusions, the development is

suppressed, and they are what remains. It's a dubious genre, suspect, and it is rather French. For me it was mostly due to my dislike of developing things.
How not to adore such a preternatural slacker?

The Great Curator. Oh, how this term has been denigrated: board games, Victorian mourning brooches, ramen, for God's sake. Cioran has re-explored nearly the whole of western (and eastern, for that matter) thought, and provided a pocket guide to its forgotten monuments, scenic vistas lost to "progress." Yes, Steiner, Queneau, Manguel, Coetzee, Henry Miller have their fans, but, would they have pointed me to Alcmaeon of Croton, Nāgārjuna, Théognis de Mégare, Fondane, Ceronetti? I don't think so.

Enough. I mentioned Knausgaard. The five books of his *My Struggle (Min Kamp)* totter on my bedside table alongside Cioran's *Oeuvres*; the two authors remain, apart from youthful flings with Kerouac and Malcolm Lowry, virtually the only complete works I have under my belt. The anti-Cioran, let's call him, Knausgaard, the man who, as James Wood, writing for the *New Yorker*, notes, is "unable to leave anything out" – shoestrings, cups of tea, the eyes of a fish, solvents, construction equipment, sketches, a teen-age New Year's Eve party (70 pages, here or there), amplifiers, the scent of graphite, a glimpse of his father urinating, on and on and on. Whereas Cioran, one concludes in short order, would like to leave *everything* out. And yet. Doesn't Woods have it just right when he goes on to say, "Knausgaard's omnivorousness proves anything but accidental…the banality is so extreme that it turns into its opposite, and becomes distinctive… hypnotic"? Couldn't the same be claimed of Cioran, his relentless intellectualism, his obsessive skepticism and tropismal melancholia so extreme it, too, eventually becomes *its* opposite – playful, almost light-fingered, hilarious – and mesmerizing? (Knausgaard and Cioran share other mirror-features, as well:

for example, the former concerned only or we can say primarily with presenting an accurate representation of himself, his physical being-in-the-world; the latter of his *thought.*) As Manguel writes, some books "call to one another" on the library shelves, for reasons known only to the reader. Such is the case, for me, with these two masters: their effects on me are mysteriously of a piece.

A bit vague, right? How to say it?

There's a marvelous poem by Ron Slate titled "Night Crossing" about a ferry ride, that begins with these words, that capture uncannily the undulative nature of (re)reading Cioran (or Knausgaard):
Back and forth is a way to move
when the visible is spacious.
For this *is* how I read Cioran: moving sideways from thought to thought, text to text, a recursive voyage that I have taken almost nightly for fifty years. (I find him best read just before sleep.) Like the passenger in the poem, my destination is so well-known as to be inconsequential. No plot whose threads I must pick up again, no capital S symbols or annoying or competing characters with their vying perspectives to inhabit or perspectives to filter. I relax, perpetually in a *transeat a familar*, assured of missing nothing of importance, nothing that will not reappear again, anyway, elsewhere, only slightly altered. Just the two of us, in the dark. Here or there the occasional sense of a new (as opposed to remembered) discovery, perhaps – an epiphany, but so fleeting I wonder if it existed at all –
wings seen, instantly gone,
As the poem has it.
And throughout, the silent *perceived* voice of Cioran, exhausted, vital: that disembodied soliloquy that Slate conjures exquisitely (though of course utterly unaware of my subject) that is like

the parting waters [that] make the sound of a god
murmuring for both the first and last time.

D.H. LAWRENCE'S
THREE ITALIAN TRAVEL BOOKS

by Ray Greenblatt

I

TWILIGHT IN ITALY

When the first book Twilight in Italy was written in 1912, Lawrence was very much involved with Frieda Weekley. They had run off to Italy together, but he mentions nothing about her throughout the entire work. She is not granted a divorce until 1914. When she and Lawrence marry in 1916 Twilight in Italy is finally published. Perhaps, pretending Frieda was not there for Lawrence gave the illusion that the people he met and scenes described were more first-hand, immediate, personal.

Lawrence was in good physical shape as shown by all the hiking he does in the rugged terrain of northern Italy. As a matter of fact, at age twenty-seven he tires fellow hikers younger than he. He says of a seventeen year-old Swiss he met, "Poor Emil was tired, more tired than I was. And his big boots had hurt his feet in the descent." (131)

Lawrence is excellent at descriptions of the northern Italian scenery: "The days go by, through the brief silence of winter, when the sunshine is so still and pure, like iced wine, and the dead leaves gleam brown, and water sounds hoarse in the ravines. It is so still and transcendent, the cypress trees poise like flames of forgotten darkness, that should have been blown out at the end of the summer. For as we have candles to light the darkness of night, so the cypresses are candles to keep the darkness aflame in the full sunshine." (68)

He is also superb in just a few well-chosen adjectives or phrases at getting inside a character: "Watching him, watching his absorbed, bestial and yet god-like crouching before the plant, as if he were the god of lower life, I somehow understood his isolation, why he did not marry. Pan and the ministers of Pan do not marry, the sylvan gods. They are single and isolated in their being." (91)

He can as well juxtapose the contradictory traits of a married couple: "There was in Paolo a subtle intelligence in feeling, a delicate appreciation of the other person. But the mind was unintelligent, he could not grasp a new order. Maria Fiori was much sharper and more adaptable to the ways of the world. Paolo had an almost glass-like quality, fine and clear and perfectly tempered; but he was also finished and brittle. Maria was very much coarser, more vulgar, but also she was more human, more fertile, with crude potentiality. His passion was too fixed in its motion, hers too loose and overwhelming." (72)

An intriguing point to note is that Lawrence can sound like Hemingway! Rather, since Lawrence was writing this book in 1912 and Hemingway's first collection of stories In Our Time did not come out until 1924, that first statement should be reversed. It has been said that Lawrence could overwrite in purple prose. But the spectrum of his style is broad. Notice the word choice, structure, and tone in the following passage: "So I went to bed, in the silent, wooden house. I had a small bedroom, clean and wooden and very cold. Outside, the stream was rushing. I covered myself with a great depth of feather-bed, and looked at the stars, and the shadowy upper world, and went to sleep. In the morning I washed in the ice-cold water, and was glad to set out. An icy mist was over the noisy stream, there were a few meager, shredded pine trees. I had breakfast and paid my bill: it was seven francs, more than I could afford. But that did not matter, once I was out in the air." (128)

In Lawrence's novels his characters are passionate. Yet you are never sure what the writer really thinks, let alone feels. Conversely in these Italian books Lawrence is very much in the scene; this is a valuable element in a travel book: "The way he sank on the table in exhaustion, drinking his milk, his will, nevertheless, so perfect and unblemished, triumphant through his body was broken and in anguish, was almost too much to bear. My heart was wrung for my countryman, wrung till it bled." (122)

And again about an Italian: "But I did not want him to go on: I didn't want to answer. I could feel a new spirit in him, something strange and pure and slightly frightening. He wanted something which was beyond me. And my soul was somewhere in tears, crying helplessly like an infant in the night. I could not respond: I could not answer." (114)

So far you might have sensed some intimations of angst in passages from Twilight in Italy. The "twilight" is the rise of industrialization which is Lawrence's major theme in this book. Wordsworth had written about pollution of both water and air in a sonnet as early as 1800. One hundred years later pollution had steadily increased, but pockets of what Lawrence deems "natural living" still remain. Lawrence shouts warnings many times in different ways:
"Having arrived at the one extreme of mechanical selflessness, we immediately embrace the other extreme of the transcendent Self. But we try to be both at once." (36)
"There it lay, vast masses of rough-hewn knowledge, vast masses of machines and appliances, vast masses of ideas and methods, and nothing done with it." (46)

"It is the hideous rawness of the world of men, the horrible, desolating harshness of the advance of the industrial world upon the world of nature that is so painful." (124)

"It was a sort of grief that this continent all beneath was so unreal, false, non-existent in its activity. Out of the silence one looked down on it, and it seemed to have lost all importance, all significance." (127)

"It seems to happen when the peasant suddenly leaves his home and becomes a workman. Then an entire change comes over everyone. Life is now a matter of selling oneself to slave-work, building roads or labouring in quarries or mines or on the railways, purposeless, meaningless, really slave-work, each integer doing his mere labour, and all for no purpose, except to have money, and to get away from the old system." (133)

I posit that in another hundred years, 2013, Lawrence would be amazed that mankind even still exists!

SEA AND SARDINIA

It is now nine years later, 1921, after Twilight in Italy had been written. The Lawrences had later traveled back to England during World War I. They returned first to Germany in 1920 then to Italy, specifically Sicily, in the following year. If you observe a map, Corsica is an island owned by France sitting in the Mediterranean below the border between France and Italy. Sardinia, owned by Italy, is an island below Corsica; it is only after World War II that Sardinia became a republic.

Frieda appears distinctly in this travel book. We can presume that Lawrence wanted to show a couple's—instead of just one person's—responses to foreign places. However, seldom does Lawrence show their intimacy. When upset by poor accommodations that he loses his temper, she says: "Why are you so indignant! Anyone would think your moral self had been outraged! Why take it morally? You petrify that man at the inn by the very way you speak to him, such condemnation! Why don't you take it as it comes? It's all life." (230)

In a more gentle moment: "In a sheltered place I lit the spirit lamp, and put on water to boil. The water we had taken from the cabin. Then we sat alone in the darkness, on a seat which had its back against the deck cabins, now appropriated by the staff. A thin, cold wind was travelling. We wrapped the one plaid round us both and snugged together, waiting for the tea to boil." (298)

As all these three travel books illustrate, Lawrence is on the move. But he offers no clear reason for it: "Not to be any more like a donkey with a log on its leg, fastened to weary earth that has no answer now. But to be off." (181) Sometimes he blames the place itself like Sicily: "Perhaps it is she one must flee from. At any rate, one must go: and at once. After having come back only at the end of October, already one must dash away. And it is only the third of January. And one cannot afford to move. Yet there you are: at the Etna bidding one goes." (142) This trip will include the sea voyages from Sicily to Sardinia and the return.

We discover Lawrence's major theme in this second book because Sardinia represents for him a land unspoiled by nineteenth and twentieth century materialism. "Sardinia, which has no history, no date, no race, no offering." (143) "This Sunday morning, seeing the frost among the tangled, still savage bushes of Sardinia, my soul thrilled again. This was not all known. This was not all worked out." (251)

He finds many admirable traits in the Sardinians: "Nobody about, free access to anywhere and everywhere, as usual: testifying again to Sardinian honesty." (265) "I found them almost the only really well-bred people I have met. They did not show off in any way at all, not even a show of simplicity." (261) The countryside had a positive influence on the inhabitants: "But it was a wonderful place. Usually, the life-level is reckoned as sea-level. But here, in the heart of Sardinia, the life-level is high on the golden-lit plateau." (255)

Lawrence continues to employ varied writing techniques. This second book comprises chapters but within each chapter are many sections as in a diary or notebook. He sometimes writes in fragments: "Very dark under the great carob tree as we go down the steps. Dark still the garden. Scent of mimosas, and then of jasmine. The lovely mimosa tree invisible. Dark the stony path." (145) He effectively repeats to catch the ship's motion: "And so we steam out. And almost at once the ship begins to take a long, slow, dizzy dip, and a fainting swoon upwards, and a long, slow, dizzy dip slipping away from beneath one." (164)

Sometimes he writes one long elegant sentence, as the sea voyage begins: "The sunny Ionian sea, the changing jewel of Calabria, like a fire-opal moved in the light; Italy and the panorama of Christmas clouds, night with the dog-star laying a long, luminous gleam across the sea, as if baying at us, Orion marching above; how the dog-star Sirius looks at one, looks at one! He is the hound of heaven, green, glamorous and fierce!—and then oh regal evening-star, hung westward flaring over the jagged dark precipices of tall Sicily: then Etna, that wicked witch, resting her thick white snow under the heaven, and slowly, slowly rolling her orange-coloured smoke." (141)

Much more humor is evident in this book out of all three travel books, whether it be gentle or biting. "Lemon trees, like Italians, seem to be happiest when they are touching one another all round." (147) "Insert myself like the meat in a sandwich into the tight lower bunk." (181) "Away goes the soup and appears a massive yellow omelette, like some log of bilious wood." (169)

"They look at one another, the elder ones, and laugh and comment, while the two young ones mix themselves and the table into a lemon-milk-orange-tea-sugar-biscuit-cake-chocolate mess. This inordinate Italian amiable patience with their young monkeys is astonishing." (177)

Lawrence voices many truths about himself and life. "I used to think there was no absolute evil. Now I know there is a great deal. So much that it threatens life altogether. That ghastly abstractness of criminals. They don't know any more what other people feel. Yet some horrible force drives them." (149) "After all, I am no more than a single human man wandering my lonely way across these years." (185)

We are left with some intriguing questions. Lawrence says to some Sardinian friends he made: "We promised to come back in the summer, when it was warmer. Then we should all meet again." (274) But the Lawrences never did. Another young friend asks: "You will find me a post in England, when you go in the summer?" . . . "If I can, said I. But it is not easy." (291) Did Lawrence ever follow through on his promise?

A final observation is in order. By 1921 D.H. Lawrence had published many major works: Sons and Lovers, The Rainbow, Studies in Classic American Literature, Women in Love. And yet he met again and again situations as this: "What were we, where did we come from, where were we going, why were we going, had we any children, did we want any, etc." (169) Can you imagine if a professional critic then—or today —would have been able to meet Lawrence and question him like that?!

SKETCHES OF ETRUSCAN PLACES

Each one of D.H. Lawrence's travel books has a different approach, a different theme. It had been seven years since he wrote Sea and Sardinia. In Sketches of Etruscan Places, Lawrence travels with an artist friend Earl Brewster. Brewster is only vaguely outlined; we know Frieda was with Lawrence but again she is non-existent. Perhaps he suppressed his traveling partners so the foreign setting and his commentary could be highlighted.

In the seven years between those two books Lawrence was diagnosed with TB, nearly died, and would die just three years after this book was written. And yet on the surface you would never know it from his attitude: "We trudge on along the dull road. After all, it is only five miles and a bit." (333) "He said it would be difficult. I said, then we could walk: it was only five miles, eight kilometers." (404)

In those intervening years Lawrence had written all of his major work and with Frieda had traveled round the world to now Sri Lanka, Australia, the Americas. He makes a number of references: "The rather horrible feeling of the great pyramid places in Mexico, Teotihuacan and Cholula, and Mitla in the south; or the amiably idolatrous Buddha places in Ceylon." (338) In the U.S.: "When I say ravine, don't expect a sort of Grand Canyon." (337) "This was evidently the grand avenue of the necropolis, like the million-dollar cemetery in New Orleans." (338)

Lawrence has his moments, as in the previous two travel books, when he vividly describes people he meets. For example, a morose German: "Doesn't think much of any place; doesn't think much of the Etruscans—nich viel wert; doesn't, apparently, think much of me; knows a professor or two whom I have met; knows the tombs of Tarquinia very well, having been here, and stayed here, twice before; doesn't think much of them; is going to Greece; doesn't expect to think much of it." (387)

A young man working at an inn is brought to life by how Lawrence captures his voice: "Albertino gives little grunts, like commas and semi-colons, which I write as er!—Bread they want, er?—er!—they take the little book,--here he takes an imaginary little book, lays it on the table-cloth, wets his finger and turns over the imaginary leaves—bread!—er!—p— you look under p—er!—ecco! pane!—pane!—si capisce!— bread! they want bread." (385)

However, in this travel book Lawrence is primarily focused on the Etruscan tombs in order to learn about the Etruscan people who seem to hold a secret that fascinates him. Etruria is a region just north of Rome along the west coast of Italy. Roughly a thousand years before Christ the Etruscans settled here. "There was never an etruscan nation: only, in historical times, a great league of tribes or nations using the etruscan language and the etruscan script—at least officially—and uniting in their religious feeling and observances. The Etruscan alphabet seems to have been borrowed from the old Greeks." (347)

The Romans imputed the Etruscans with a bad reputation. Lawrence states sarcastically: "However, those pure, clean-living, sweet-souled Romans, who smashed nation after nation and crushed the free soul in people after people, and were ruled by Messalina and Heliogabalus and such-like snowdrops, they said the Etruscans were vicious." (332) But Lawrence proves that the Etruscans were equal in power to the Romans yet more humane.

"The Etruscans built everything of wood, house, temples, all save walls for fortification, great gates, bridges, and drainage works. So that the Etruscan cities vanished as completely as flowers." (335) Their wealth could be measured by observing the Etruscan city of Cerveteri: "We can have an idea of the vast mass of wealth this city could afford to bury with its dead, in days when Rome had very little gold, and even bronze was precious." (340) They were also great sailors: "Yet this is the Tyrrhenian sea of the Etruscans, where their shipping spread sharp sails, and beat the sea with slave-oars, roving in from Greece and Sicily." (345)

However, the true secret of the Etruscans ironically for Lawrence lay in their vast underground tombs. And he explores many, to name just a few, the Tomb of: the Old Man, Maiden, Lionesses, Feast, Leopards, Hunting and Fishing, Shields, Baron, Bulls, Dead Man, etc. In these many tombs was writing: "Little sentences freely written in red paint, or scratched in the stucco with the finger, slanting with the real Etruscan carelessness and fullness of life." (340) There were drawings as well: "The low relief carvings and stucco reliefs on the pillars and the walls round the burial niches." (340) Drawings represented, in part: shields, helmets, swords, spears, necklace, scepter, dog, lions, goose, etc.

In a sarcophagus would be "the Lucumo (chieftain) and the sacred treasures of the dead, the little bronze ship of death that would bear him over to the other world, the vases of jewels for his arraying, the vases of small dishes, the little bronze statuettes and tools, the weapons, the armour: all the amazing impedimenta of the important dead. Or sometimes, in the inner room, lay the woman, the great lady, in all her robes, with the mirror in her hand, and her treasures, her jewels and combs and silver boxes of cosmetics, in urns or vases ranged alongside." (339)

By now Lawrence had discovered the secret of the Etruscans. "The underworld of the Etruscans was a gay place." (364) "Once it was all bright and dancing; the delight of the underworld; honouring the dead with wine and flutes playing for a dance, and limbs whirling and pressing." (372) "It is neither preaching nor teaching nor commanding nor urging. It is just singing. And in the beginning was not a Word, but a chirrup." (356) "To the Etruscan, all was alive: the whole universe lived: and the business of man was himself to live amid it all." (374)

For Lawrence "there was a stillness and a soothingness in all the air, in the sunken place, and a feeling that it was good for one's soul to be there." (338) "And gradually, the underworld of the Etruscans becomes more real than the above day of the afternoon. One begins to live with the painted dancers and feasters and mourners, and to look eagerly for them." (367) "If you love the odd spontaneous forms that are never to be standardised, go to the Etruscans." (359) "The Etruscans are not a theory or a thesis. If they are anything, they are an experience." (435)

CODA: In Twilight in Italy D.H. Lawrence hiked the mountains of northern Italy condemning the excessive materialism and mechanization he saw in the world. Throughout Sea and Sardinia, he was searching for an unspoiled people in an unspoiled land. Finally, with little time left to live, in Sketches of Etruscan Places Lawrence perhaps unconsciously within the ethos of the Etruscan tombs found an environment where his restless soul could be content.

All excerpts taken from D.H. LAWRENCE AND ITALY (Penguin Classics, 2007)

CONTRIBUTORS

Cathy Allman has a MFA in creative writing from Manhattanville College and teaches creativity workshops for a variety of schools as well as in her Connecticut office. Her work has appeared in many journals including Blue Earth Review, California Quarterly, The Potomac Review, Terminus and Town Creek Poetry.
For more, visit **CathyAllman.com**

When **Jodi Adamson** isn't dispensing happy pills or administering vaccines, she reads, writes, designs and sews costumes, and plays with her yorkiepoo and two cats. Her costumes have placed in the Alabama National Fair, and her complete, hand sewn, period authentic 1840s summer ball gown ensemble won second place in the Daughters of the American Revolution 2015 National Heritage Historical Costume Contest.

Linda Aschbrenner, Marshfield, WI, edited and published the poetry journal *Free Verse* (1998-2009) and founded Marsh River Editions in 2001, publishing 17 chapbooks for fellow poets. She is presently working on a family memoir in poetry and prose with her sisters. Her poetry, essays, book reviews, and short stories have appeared in a number of publications and anthologies, including *California Quarterly, Cats, Yankee, True Confessions, Verse Wisconsin,* and *Local Ground(s): Midwest Poetics.*

David Adès is a Pushcart Prize nominated Australian poet living in Sydney. He has won the University of Canberra Vice-Chancellor's International Poetry Prize, been shortlisted for the Newcastle Poetry Prize. In 2016 Adès was a finalist in the Alexander and Dora Raynes Poetry Prize and highly commended in the Bruce Dawe National Poetry Prize.

Cathy Barber's poetry has appeared recently in *Pinyon, SLAB* and *Kestrel* and has been anthologized many times. *Atlas and Alice* nominated her "Three Short Love Poems" for a Best of the Net award, 2015. She is a graduate of the VCFA's MFA in Writing program.

Michele Belluomini's poetry has appeared in a number of print and online journals. Her books of poetry are *Crazy Mary & Others*, and *Signposts for Sleepwalkers*. She has read at various venues throughout the city. She is Adjunct Library Faculty at Phila. Community College.

Erik Bendix's poetry distills both a silence of the woods he lives in and a vitality drawn from his family's Holocaust survival. A student of movement arts from Tai Chi to dervish whirling, he listens for how cadence resonates in the body. He has translated Rilke's complete *Duino Elegies* and *Sonnets to Orpheus*. His work has appeared in the *Asheville Poetry Review, Forge, Monarch Review, Poetry East, Spoon River Poetry Review* and *Word Riot*.

Joseph A. Chelius is a former Bucks County poet laureate. His full-length collection, *The Art of Acquiescence*, was published by WordTech Communications in 2014; new work has appeared in *Poet Lore* and *Schuylkill Valley Journal* and is forthcoming in *American Journal of Poetry*.

Mike Cohen hosts Poetry Aloud and Alive at Philadelphia's Big Blue Marble Book Store. His articles on sculpture appear in the SVJ and he is a contributing editor. His wry writing has appeared in the *Mad Poets Review, Apiary Magazine, Fox Chase Review*, and other journals. Mike's poetry can be found at **http://mikecohensays.com/** and in his book BETWEEN THE I'S.

Joan Colby has published 17 books including *Selected Poems* from FutureCycle Press which received the 2013 FutureCycle Prize and *Ribcage* from Glass Lyre Press which has been awarded the 2015 Kithara Book Prize. Her latest book *Carnival* is just out from FutureCycle Press.

Barbara Crooker is the author of eight books of poetry including *Les Fauves* (C&R Press, 2017) and *The Book of Kells* (The Poeima Poetry Series, Cascade Books, 2019). Her writing has received a number of awards, including the 2004 WB Yeats Society of New York Award, the 2003 Thomas Merton Poetry of the Sacred Award, and three Pennsylvania Council on the Arts Creative Writing Fellowships. Recently, she was in residence at the Tyrone Guthrie Centre, Ireland.

Eileen D'Angelo, Editor of *Mad Poets Review*, has poetry and book reviews published in *Rattle* and *Manhattan Poetry Review* among others. She has read poetry on WXPN World Café Live, Saint Joseph's University, Rutgers and other venues and judged open auditions for the pilot program of HBO's *Def Poetry Jam*. Director of Mad Poets since 1987, she has coordinated 1500 special events in the tri-state area.

Susanne Davis's short stories have been published in many journals including *American Short Fiction, Notre Dame Review, descant, Feminist Studies, St. Petersburg* Review, and *Zone 3*. She holds an MFA from the Iowa Writers' Workshop and teaches creative writing at Trinity College and the University of CT. She has also completed a novel called *Gravity Hill*.

George Drew is the author of **The View from Jackass Hill**, 2010 winner of the X. J. Kennedy Poetry Prize, Texas Review Press, which also published **Down & Dirty** (2015), and his New & Selected, **Pastoral Habits**, in 2016. His seventh collection, **Fancy's Orphan**, is due out in January, 2017, from Tiger Bark Press. He is the winner of the 2014 *St. Petersburg Review* poetry contest.

W. D. Ehrhart is author or editor of 21 books of prose and poetry, few of which you've ever heard. He teaches history and English at the Haverford School.

Alfred Encarnacion has taught at Temple University, published poems in *Crab Orchard Review, Florida Review, Indiana Review, North American Review,* and *The Paterson Literary Review.* His two books of poetry are *The Outskirts of Karma* and *Ambassadors of the Silenced.* He's been nominated for a Pushcart Prize; he's the director of the Stratford Public Library in New Jersey.

Joseph Farley edited Axe Factory from 1986-2010. His novel Labor Day is available from Peasantry Press. His poetry collections include *Suckers*, Cynic Press, 2005, and *Longing for the Mother Tongue*, March Street Press, 2010.

Twice a Pushcart Prize nominee and finalist in *Atlanta Review*'s 2016 International Poetry Contest, **Linda M. Fischer** has poems published or forthcoming in *the Aurorean, Ibbetson Street, Iodine Poetry Journal, Muddy River Poetry Review, Potomac Review, Roanoke Review, Valparaiso Poetry Review, Verse-Virtual,* and elsewhere. For information about her chapbooks and more poems: lindamfischer.com

John Grey is an Australian poet, US resident. Recently published in *New Plains Review, Stillwater Review* and *Big Muddy Review* with work upcoming in *Louisiana Review, Cape Rock* and *Spoon River Poetry Review.*

Ray Greenblatt has been connected with the SVJ from its inception as a poet, essayist and fiction writer. Thirty years ago he and Peter Krok, Editor-in-Chief of the SVJ, formed the Overbrook Poets. Ray Greenblatt's poetry has been translated into Gaelic, Polish and Japanese. He has a poetry collection entitled *Shadow with Green Eyes* from Meg Kennedy Press. A novel of his is *Twenty Years on Graysheep Bay*.

Luray Gross, a storyteller as well as a poet, has worked with thousands of students and teachers during her twenty-some years as an Artist in Residence. She was awarded a Fellowship in Poetry by the New Jersey State Council on the Arts and named one of their Distinguished Teaching Artists. She is the author of three collections of poetry, most recently *The Perfection of Zeros*, published by Word Tech. She lives in Bucks County, PA, a few miles from the dairy farm where she grew up.

Adele Kenny, author of 24 books, is founding director of the Carriage House Poetry series and poetry editor of *Tiferet*. Among other awards, she has received fellowships from the NJ State Arts Council, Kean University's Distinguished Alumni Award, and is a Paterson Prize finalist.

David P. Kozinski won the Delaware Literary Connection's 2015 spring poetry contest. His full-length book of poems, *Tripping Over Memorial Day* is scheduled to be published by Kelsay Press. Publications include *Apiary, Cheat River Review, Fox Chase Review, Mad Poets Review, Philadelphia Stories, Rasputin, The Rathalla Review* and *Schuylkill Valley Journal*. He is a board member of the Philadelphia Writers' Conference and of the Manayunk-Roxborough Art Center. Kozinski is the Arts Editor of the Schuylkill Valley Journal Online (**www.svjlit.com**). He has conducted poetry workshops for teens at the Montgomery County (PA) Youth Center and at

Roosevelt High School in Norristown, PA, for Expressive Path, a non-profit organization that encourages youth participation in the arts.

Peter Krok is the Humanities director of the Manayunk-Roxborough Art Center in Philadelphia where he has been coordinating literary programs since 1990. He is also Editor-in-Chief of the *Schuylkill Valley Journal* (SVJ), which was founded in 1990, and the SVJ Online at svjlit.com. He is a much-published poet and known as the "red brick poet" because of his connection with the city. His book *Looking For An Eye* was published by Foothills Press in 2008.

Matt Lake is an editorial gun for hire whose nonfiction work has appeared in the *New York Times, San Francisco Chronicle,* and *Baltimore Sun.* He has written or co-written six books in the *Weird U.S.* series, and has made several appearances on the History Channel to explain monsters and technology to a lay audience. His first published poetical works were children's folk tales translated from German.

Daniel Lawless's book, *The Gun My Sister Killed Herself With and Other Poems* is forthcoming from Salmon Poetry, February 2018. Recent poems appear or are forthcoming in *Cortland Review, B O D Y, The Common, FIELD, The Louisville Review, Ploughshares, Prairie Schooner,* and other journals. He is the founder and editor of *Plume: A Journal of Contemporary Poetry.*

Yvonne Higgins Leach is the author of *Another Autumn* (WordTech Editions, 2014). After earning a Master of Fine Arts from Eastern Washington University, she spent decades balancing a career in communications and public relations, raising a family, and pursuing her love of writing poetry.

Evalyn Lee is a former CBS News producer currently living in London with her husband and two children. Over the years, she has produced television segments for *60 Minutes* in New York and then for the BBC in London. Her broadcast work has received an Emmy and numerous Writers Guild Awards and she currently is working on her first novel.

David Livewell grew up in Kensington and won the 2012 T.S. Eliot Poetry Prize for his book, *Shackamaxon* (Truman State University Press).

Born and raised in Missouri, **Roger Lopata** has lived in the Philadelphia area for most of the last 40 years. His writing has appeared in various publications including *Alabama Literary Review, Chesapeake Bay Magazine, New Millennium Writings, Other Voices, Nimrod, Painted Bride Quarterly, Sou'wester, Sail,* and *The Worcester Review.*

Cobber 'Stumpy' Malloy imagines himself as a man from the bush but in fact has rarely left suburbia, a fact that his constant wearing of an Akubra hat and boots cannot hide. Biographical details are sketchy but he may not be who he says he is.

Carla McGill and her husband live in Southern California, where she earned a doctorate in literature from the University of California, Riverside. Her work has been published in *Shark Reef, Crack the Spine, Westview, Common Ground Review, Caveat Lector, Vending Machine Press,* and elsewhere.

Lisa Meckel, a presenter for NEA's The Big Read, honoring poet Robinson Jeffers, has been published in various journals including *Nimrod, Rattle, Reed Magazine, Mirboo North Times, Victoria Australia* and *Carmel Valley News.* She is currently preparing her first collection.

Joyce Meyers' poems have appeared in *The Atlanta Review, The Comstock Review, Iodine Poetry Journal,* and *Slant.* She has two chapbooks, *Wild Mushrooms* (Plan B Press, 2007) and *Shapes of Love* (Finishing Line Press, 2010). Her full-length volume of poems, *The way back,* is forthcoming from Aldrich Press.

Elise A. Miller's fiction appears in *Northern Liberties Review, Elephant Journal, Wild River Review* and *Schuylkill Valley Journal.* She has written articles for WomansDay.com and PopSugar.com. Her novel *Star Craving Mad* was released in 2015, followed by *Tracing the Bones* in 2016. Elise lives in Havertown with her husband, two kids and two teeny rescue dogs.

Eileen Moeller has an M.A. in Creative Writing from Syracuse University, and poems in *Ars Medica, Feminist Studies, Paterson Literary Review, Blue Fifth Review,* and *Philadelphia Stories.* Her two books are: *Firefly, Brightly Burning* and *The Girls In Their Iron Shoes.*

Robert Brian Mulder taught English in Papua New Guinea, Israel, and North Carolina. He is currently working as a writing tutor at The Catlin Gabel School in Portland, Oregon.

Julie Murphy, adjunct professor at JFK University, teaches poetry as a volunteer at the Salinas Valley State Prison. A member of the Academy of American Poets, her work is published or forthcoming in *CALYX Journal, Crack the Spine* and *Pennsylvania English.*

Dale Ritterbusch is the author of *Lessons Learned: Poetry of the Vietnam War and Its Aftermath* and *Far From the Temple of Heaven.* He recently retired as a Professor of English at the University of Wisconsin-Whitewater and twice served as

Distinguished Visiting Professor at the United States Air Force Academy.

Hayden Saunier is the author of *Tips for Domestic Travel, Say Luck* (2013 Gell Poetry Prize), and *Field Trip to the Underworld*, (Keystone Chapbook Award). Her work has been awarded the Pablo Neruda Prize, the Rattle Poetry Prize, the Robert Fraser Award as well as a Bucks County, Pennsylvania Poet Laureateship.

Joseph Howard Tyson, a native of Germantown, graduated from LaSalle University in 1969 with a B.A. in Philosophy. He has worked in the insurance industry since 1972, and still lives in the Philadelphia area. He has written six non-fiction books: *Penn's Luminous City, Madam Blavatsky Revisited, Hitler's Mentor, The Surreal Reich, World War II Leaders*, and *Fifty-Seven Years of Russian Madness*.

Michael Dylan Welch lives near Seattle, co-founded the American Haiku Archives and the Haiku North America biennial conference, and founded National Haiku Writing Month (**nahaiwrimo.com**). His poems and essays have appeared in hundreds of journals and anthologies. Michael's latest books are *Becoming a Haiku Poet* and *Off the Beaten Track*. His website is **graceguts.com**.

Helen Wickes has four books of poetry: *In Search of Landscape*, 2007, published by Sixteen Rivers Press; *Moon Over Zabriskie* and *Dowser's Apprentice*, both from Glass Lyre Press in 2014; *World as You Left It*, 2015, from Sixteen Rivers Press.

Robert Zaller is Distinguished University Professor of History at Drexel University. His most recent books are *Speaking to Power* and *Robinson Jeffers and the American Sublime*.

Schuylkill Valley Journal

—Submission Guidelines—

The *Schuylkill Valley Journal* is published as both a print and online journal. The SVJ Print is released twice a year, in spring and fall. The SVJ Online (svjlit.com) is published on a more frequent basis. The SVJ publishes short stories, flash fiction, interviews, photography, citscapes, critical essays and features on art and sculpture (especially Philadelphia sculpture). The SVJ also publishes poetry; however, all poetry will first appear in the Print SVJ.

All submissions should be sent though the online website **svj.query@gmail.com**, We prefer previously unpublished work though published work is acceptable (indicate where previously published). Simultaneous submissions are OK (please notify us if your work is published elsewhere). All submissions will be considered for both our print and online journals. Our aim in reviewing material that is first considered for the SVJ Online (material other than poetry and longer short stories) is to inform writers of the status of their inquiry within two weeks.

Submissions should be sent in .doc or .rtf file format only in Times New Roman, 12 point font, and single-spaced and should include title, author name, bio and complete text, including any notes regarding previous publication. In the subject line all submissions should state the submission type (*eg.* short story, flash fiction, poetry) and include the writer's full name and contact information. Any file not meeting these specifications may not be read. Manuscripts will not be returned. All submissions except poetry should include a word count.

Poetry: Send 3-5 poems. Submit poetry to **svjpoetry@yahoo.com** in the body of an email. The poetry co-editors are Bernadette McBride and Bill Wunder. If for some reason you are unable to submit via email, poetry can also be submitted via the SVJ website (svjlit.com).

Short Stories and Flash Fiction: 1-2 stories (if more than 3,000 words please only submit 1). Flash fiction (preferably 500-1,000 words); short stories (no more than 6,000 words). Submissions will be considered for both the online and print journal, with the exception of short stories greater than 2,000 words (Print SVJ only). We like fiction that tells a story or illuminates a character. We look for original use of language, fresh voices and diversity. We also seek writers who have insights into the mysteries of everyday life, relationships and the world around us. Stories can pose questions and answer them or not; however, they must be well-crafted. Stories can be sent through the online website at **svj.query@gmail.com**, or can be sent via snail mail. The preferred method is via snail mail. Stories sent by snail mail should be typed, double-spaced, one side only with name, address, word count and bio on first page. Send to:

Fran Metzman
Fiction Editor, Schuylkill Valley Journal
1900 JFK Blvd, /2012
Philadelphia, PA 19103

Essays and Interviews: 5,000 words max. (preferably under 2,000 words for the SVJ Online) on topics of literary or artistic interest, personal reflections, interviews, etc. Submissions should incude the word count and bio on first page. Inquiry to email address (macpoet1@aol.com) is always advisable. Queries should include a concept/abstract of the proposed article, approximately a paragraph. All submissions will be sent through **query.svj@gmail.com**. All articles and non-fiction pieces will be assigned by editor.

Schuylkill Valley Journal

—Copyright—

Material that appears in the *Schuylkill Valley Journal* (Print and Online) is the copyright of the contributor. By submitting a work to the SVJ, the contributor agrees that the *Schuylkill Valley Journal* reserves first rights and the right to retain the material in our archives indefinitely. It may also be used in reference to previous issues and be included in future SVJ endeavors. All other rights belong to the contributor. The SVJ Online does not claim ownership of syndicated material from other sources, and proper credit will be given as necessary. We request the same courtesy from our peers. All rights are similarly reserved by the Schuylkill Valley Journal.

—Payment—

For contributors to the SVJ Print, payment is 1 copy of the journal in which your work appears. Additional copies are $9 each. All rights revert to authors upon publication. The cost of the Schuylkill Valley Journal is $10 an issue and $13 if sent via mail. For other information about the journal, contact Peter Krok, the publisher and Editor-in-Chief of the SVJ and Humanities Director of the Manayunk-Roxborough Art Center (MRAC), at macpoet1@aol.com or by phone at 215-482-3363.

Subscription Form –
Schuylkill Valley Journal

Name: _____

Street Address: _____

City, State, Zip Code: _____

Phone: _____

Subscriptions: ( ) One Year $23*   ( ) Two Years $45*
              (includes postage)   (includes postage)

For an issue that contains my work:
( ) Send my payment copies with my subscription copy.
( ) Send my payment copies and transfer my subscription to the next issue.

Contributions
( ) $10   ( ) $20   ( ) $25   ( ) $50   ( ) $Other

Please make checks payable to Peter Krok – Schuylkill Valley Journal and mail to: Peter Krok, 240 Golf Hills Road, Havertown, PA 19083

*For subscriptions that do not require postage a one year subscription is $20 and a two year subscription is $40.